THE NECESSITY OF SUNDAY SCHOOLS

THE NECESSITY OF SUNDAY SCHOOLS

IN THIS POST-CHRISTIAN ERA

PETER MASTERS
& MALCOLM H. WATTS

THE WAKEMAN TRUST * LONDON

THE NECESSITY OF SUNDAY SCHOOLS

© Peter Masters & Malcolm H. Watts 1992
First published 1992

THE WAKEMAN TRUST
Elephant & Castle
London SE1 6SD

ISBN 1 870855 13 2

Cover design by Andrew Sides

Printed in Great Britain by J. W. Arrowsmith of Bristol

Contents

*Chapters 1, 2, 3, 5 and 7 are by Peter Masters, and
chapters 4 and 6 are by Malcolm H. Watts*

1. The Unique Virtues of Sunday Schools

SUNDAY SCHOOLS, when operated with vision, vigour and evangelistic purpose, achieve great things, and their distinctive virtues ought to be appreciated and extolled. Like no other agency they enable us to reach a large part of the rising generation, and to draw children and teenagers to the Saviour.

Indeed, whether or not a congregation contains young people saved from the neighbourhood will usually depend on whether there has been an effective Sunday School, coupled with teenage Bible Classes. The general rule is – no Sunday School ministry, no saved teens and twenties in the church, except, perhaps, for children of believers, and those converted in some other church. It is as predictable and inevitable as that!

But aside from its evangelistic purpose, the Sunday

School is also a vital ministry of warning. We must not forget that we have a dual ministry, because God has determined that His mercy and His love will be declared to all so that those who reject Him shall, in the last day, be without excuse. We are to warn and teach everyone *(Colossians 1.28)*.

In our Sunday Schools we are not only toiling for the salvation of children and young people, but we are also tenderly and clearly warning them. It is both a ministry of redemption and a ministry of warning on a large scale!

However, there are other special and glorious attributes of Sunday Schools which we should value very highly. For example, Sunday Schools *protect* the young like no other agency on earth. They gather young people in from the community and rescue them from the foul rape of the mind carried out by this present world. They deliver children from the murder of their souls, ruthlessly perpetuated by an evil, arrogant, apostate age. They snatch young lives from the pain and injury of the permissive society. May God so bless our Sunday Schools that children and teenagers shall grow up – even if not yet saved – unscathed from the worst excesses of moral experiment and sin!

We have seen great deliverances arising from this aspect of Sunday School ministry. Throughout this land many former Sunday School and Bible Class children have embarked upon young adulthood possessing a spiritual training which has not yet had its impact on their lives. Then, just as they have been about to launch into some moral excess, something has stopped them! What they have heard from God's Word has restrained their minds and hearts, and enabled them to see the futility and immorality of the route they were about to take. We have heard of those who have been suddenly sickened as they were about to immerse themselves in some utterly godless, blasphemous and sensual activity. Their Sunday School background held them back, and the Holy Spirit used it to bring them under conviction.

We see the same divine handiwork in the annals of Christian biography, where godless men and women have suddenly heard again – in their hearts – long-forgotten elements of childhood instruction. It is a melting privilege to be able to put a shield of Truth around the young to protect them from the rape and mutilation of sin.

In the communities around our churches there are countless young people who are being subjected at this very moment to the most savage anti-Christian brain-washing, and only the Sunday School can help them. It delivers children from being duped by this present world, and from being spiritually maimed and hurt.

The Sunday School is wonderful in another respect also. Nothing ducks under the devil's defences like the old-fashioned Sunday School. Notice how it gets round the fortified walls of Satan! In communities where there is a high degree of drug abuse, alcoholism, crime, and hatred of the things of God, it is immensely difficult for church visitors to get into homes, and to speak in a credible way to adults. How can we reach such homes? What can we do? How may we overcome the barriers and the antagonism in our community? The fortifications of the devil are seemingly impregnable.

Yet the marvellous thing about an old-fashioned Sunday School is that its influence goes right under the walls which Satan has erected. Sunday Schools may reach into all kinds of homes. When we visit for the children we are invariably successful, and they come tumbling out to attend the house of God.

Parents who would slam the door if the visit was an effort to reach *them*, will send their children, and then the parents will gradually become more sympathetic. Older brothers and sisters, even those unreachable through addiction to current teenage idols, or even to drugs, may one day be touched, because the church cares for the little ones, and has developed a credible contact with their homes.

How often we have heard testimonies to the unique and remarkable agency of Sunday Schools! Today, the Sunday School is still the greatest spiritual and social blessing to needy children. In some of our toughest urban communities there are children whose *only* contact with genuine kindness, sympathy and affection, is at Sunday School. And this is *often* the case.

This is the greatest *social* work we can be engaged in. We have children today who are beaten, cursed, never loved, and even abused, and whose lifeline to sanity and to people of character is through the child evangelism ministry. In their Sunday School, Bible Class, and weeknight meeting staffs, they have friends who relate to them and are concerned for them. May God help His people to see once again the wonderful merits and opportunities of Sunday Schools!

Can we not draw the teenagers into our church? Is it impossible to attract them in any number to the Gospel services? The reason is, we have no 'fishers'! And we have no fishers because we have no effective Sunday School ministry to *outside* children.

It is the fruit of the Sunday School which provides enthusiastic teenage fishers, and just *one* such keen, zealous youngster will fill a room. May God grant us such fishers, so that young people of Bible Class age, and up into late teens and early twenties, may be found in our congregations, seeking the Lord.

Aside from its soul-saving, soul-protecting, and soul-warning ministry, the Sunday School also blesses the *adult* church in a deeply significant way. It does this, firstly, by providing important avenues of service for all.

The writer was saddened and surprised some years ago to read in a Christian magazine an article by a Christian woman who complained that there was nothing for women to do in evangelical churches. Yet, as Luther pointed out, a woman has more wisdom and power for teaching and handling children in her little finger than the average man in his whole body.

In the Sunday School we have the most urgent and profitable ministry imaginable, and usually we have insufficient people to fulfil it on the necessary scale. Why have our Sunday Schools closed when they provide such important and fulfilling avenues of service for *all* the Lord's people?

The Sunday School, as an employer of the gifts of saved people, is a most effective channel of personal assurance. Why do the people of God sometimes lack assurance of salvation? The reason, so often, is because the Sunday School is too small. What has this to do with assurance? The answer is that if God's people were labouring in the work of the Sunday School, visiting the children, teaching the young, pouring out their hearts in intercession before the Lord for ever increasing numbers and for conversions, and also praying for personal strength and blessing, they would be *so much in touch with God,* and receiving *so many wonderful answers* to their prayers, that they would no longer have an assurance problem. If we have a large Sunday School, then we have many of the members of our fellowship in service, and it is through such service that believers prove the Lord.

Sunday Schools also yield up many 'incidental'

benefits to the churches. They are, for example, a most effective means of identifying (or disqualifying) and training future preachers. In fact, Sunday Schools are arguably the best schools for preachers which could possibly be devised.

Show us a man who wants to declaim importantly, but who is not interested in young souls. He cannot speak plain, engaging, understandable English, and he cannot adjust to different kinds of hearer. He has never struggled to address children or teenagers, or to put things simply and plainly. Such a man would be no use in the ministry, and the Sunday School will reveal that with almost ruthless efficiency.

On the other hand, the Sunday School will draw attention to those who are really *apt to teach*, and then prove them in stickability and largeness of heart.

Think, also, of how the Sunday School commends a church to its neighbourhood. Even hardened cynics will often begin to think, 'Well, they do a lot for the children,' and develop a soft spot for the church, and greater openness to its approaches.

It is the writer's experience of nearly thirty years ago that even a powerful county authority may be moved to extend land and favours because a pioneer church has built a large Sunday School in the community.

Then, finally, who knows what blessing and instrumentality may be given to a church in its adult outreach *on account of* its faithfulness to the rising generation in its community? For did not the Lord say, *He that is faithful in that which is least is faithful also in much (Luke 16.10)*?

Sunday Schools, without doubt, are not only the best but generally the *only* feasible means of reaching large numbers of children in our communities, and they still have unique strengths. Have we allowed our appreciation of this ministry to become eroded? Have we lost sight of the opportunities and possibilities?

2. Why Have so Many Sunday Schools Closed?

IN *MATTHEW 18.14* we are given some very remarkable words by our Saviour – words which should stir our minds to deep wonder at the heart of God – *Even so it is not the will of your Father which is in heaven, that one of these little ones should perish.* This wonderful and astonishing statement assures us that the Lord's heart is *for* the children.

There is an oft-told anecdote from the life of Luther that at one stage in the Reformation, when things were going very badly, Luther and Melancthon walked into a room where they found children praying for them. One or the other of them (and I suspect it was Luther rather than Melancthon) exclaimed, 'It is well, for the children are praying for us. God will be sure to hear them!' The Reformers knew the heart of Almighty God.

The work of the Spirit among children is a profound matter. The Lord, we know, chooses the weak things of the world to confound the things which are mighty.

This is the God Who, in a time of Israel's dire national emergency, when the cause of Truth was at a low ebb, and when the representative and spokesman of the Word had failed, took a *child* named Samuel, revealed Himself to him, flooded him with spiritual light, and appointed him as His chosen instrument for a glorious season of deliverance and blessing! Truly, these are deep things!

As we focus our minds on the issue of young people's and children's work, let us be aware that we are treading, as it were, on holy ground, and we must think reverently, carefully and deeply.

One of the great problems now assailing the ministry of Sunday Schools is that many churches are entertaining grave doubts about the biblical validity of this work. The very existence of the Sunday School is being questioned, and friends are asking – 'Where is the scriptural warrant?' Indeed, it is confidently asserted that children's Sunday Schools are a *human* innovation. However, the warrant for child evangelism, and therefore for Sunday Schools, is explicit and strong, but it certainly needs to be articulated again in these days.

A biblical commission is primarily given in order that it should be obeyed, but it also happens to be the greatest possible inspiration, stimulation and encouragement for those who do obey. After all, if *the Lord* has commanded that something be done, then it is plainly His sovereign and perfect will, and He will bless it. If, therefore, we are convinced that there is a biblical warrant for child evangelism, then we will be filled with strong patience, resilience and enthusiasm through all the arduous labour and the set-backs involved. Knowing that our sphere of service is God's chosen work, we will work with great fervour and faithfulness.

The fact that the biblical warrant for the evangelisation of the young has not been articulated in recent years is surely a great mystery. It is amazing that well-rehearsed principles from the past can disappear from view so quickly! Do those friends who contend against child evangelism really know so little about the teaching of our Reformation, Puritan and Victorian forebears?

However, before setting out the biblical authority for teaching God's standards and the Gospel to the young, it is important that we should look with alarm at the dramatic decline in this ministry during this century, and particularly since the Second World War. Many younger ministers and church leaders do not appreciate the enormous scale of the loss of Sunday Schools.

A steep decline certainly set in at the beginning of the century, and for the first forty years Sunday Schools experienced reduced attendances. Nevertheless, until World War II, children's outreach was still vastly greater and more wonderful than it has been since, and we must be aware of this. At the Metropolitan Tabernacle, for example, in the pre-war years the church regarded its Sunday School ministry as being in a state of tragic decline. The workers lamented the times, and grieved at the languishing state of their departments. They were appalled at the reduction in numbers over the preceding thirty years. But how many children did they have in this Sunday School which they reckoned to be in a condition of decline? They had more than 1500 children; and that, to them, was grievously disappointing!

They likewise wept over the state of the branch missions, one of which had a Sunday School roll which would today top the league for the entire UK. Another of the smaller missions was compelled to operate its Sunday School in shifts, because the premises were not large enough for all the children. Yet all this was regarded with disappointment, because their minds went back to earlier days.

In very many towns and cities the situation was the same. Sunday Schools, though much smaller than in the previous century, were always extremely large measured by today's standards.

The writer firmly believes that one of the reasons why public morality was maintained in this country until the early sixties, despite the demise of spiritual life, was the extraordinary work of Sunday Schools. The last great fruit of large Sunday Schools was the maintaining of standards of reverence and decency throughout the 1940s and 1950s, until the dawn of the permissive society in the 1960s. Only then were people induced by a reprehensible media to throw off moral restraint. The abandonment of standards had to wait for the rise of an uninhibited generation which, by and large, had not been to Sunday School.

In the post-war period Sunday Schools never achieved pre-war figures, although *some* effort remained, so that in the early 1960s the Sunday School anniversary was still the highlight of many a church calendar. On that day the average church would be crowded with children and parents, and there would be special evangelistic anniversary meetings. Now, however, the Sunday School anniversary of so many churches is a pathetic affair. All this is a history of collapse which should fill us with profound shock and dismay, but strangely, it disturbs us hardly at all.

In considering this subject, two tragedies, not one, should be brought into focus. Not only have Sunday Schools closed or diminished in size to an appalling degree, but also the *distinctive vision* of Sunday Schools has entirely gone, even where schools exist. Virtually no one today thinks as our forebears used to think, grasping the original objective of the Sunday School.

As far as this writer knows, there is nothing in print today advancing and encouraging the vision of Sunday Schooling as it was held from the flowering of the

Sunday School movement right up until the Second World War.

The original vision or aim of Sunday Schools was nothing short of this: to reach (as God enabled) *whole communities* of children and young people, and to be responsible for the spiritual and moral training and protection of an entire generation. Who holds and implements such a vision of Sunday Schools today?

Do those of us who are pastors have our sights lifted any higher than simply to provide instruction for the children of church members, plus a privileged few from the neighbourhood around the church?

Do we react away from a large Sunday School out-reach, protesting, 'We could not entertain such a vision because our church premises are not large enough'? What we ought to say, of course, is, 'In order to accom-modate a realistic number of children we will have to hire a day-school to supplement our own premises.'

In our day we must rediscover and accept the burden of responsibility to reach, if the Lord enables, *entire communities* of young people in order to train and warn them. This is the true purpose of Sunday Schooling, and it is the loss of this outlook which has led to the shrinkage and closure of so many schools, and the con-sequent failure of evangelical churches to seriously influence each rising generation since the Second World War.

Prior to the United Kingdom general election in

April 1992, *The Spectator* magazine carried an article about the leaders of the main political parties, pointing out that for the first time in modern history *none* of the candidates for the premiership possessed any orthodox Christian training or commitment – even of the most nominal kind.

One of these leaders defined faith as a synonym for personal values. Another felt that the only worthwhile features in Christianity were a number of social ethics.

The third took a curious view, akin to New Age philosophy, believing that humanity is in the course of an evolutionary process. Ultimately, it will not need leaders or bureaucratic structures because the race will advance to the point where intuitive insight will analyse and solve all problems, and people will then live harmoniously together.

When such prominent men (in common with the overwhelming majority of people in British public life) have no understanding whatsoever of the elements of biblical Christianity, it confirms that we are now in the post-Christian age! But who or what is to blame for the demise of biblical Christianity in our land?

We evangelicals are very good at sighing, and bemoaning the state of the times, but we do not have very broad shoulders. We never take responsibility. We are never heard saying, 'This has come about because we have shut down the Sunday Schools, or left them at a minimal level of operation. This has happened because we have retreated into a small-thinking manner of carrying out our witness. It is because we have not been interested in reaching the entire community. *We* are to blame.'

If a church is in a state of terminal collapse, or if the children's meetings have closed, no fault will ever be assigned to anyone. Why is evangelical Christianity now an obscure, unknown message in places both high and low? 'O, it is society's fault! It is the godlessness of the people! It is the immorality of television entertainment and the atheism of modern education!' These are the answers we give.

The truth, however, behind the collapse of Sunday Schools is that the pastors are to blame; the elders are to blame; the deacons are to blame, and church members are to blame. Where are the Sunday Schools? *Why* are whole generations of youngsters in each neighbourhood no longer channelled through evangelistic ministry and Bible teaching in Sunday Schools? What has gone wrong and what has happened?

The answer is that the pastors lost interest in them, the elders did not strive to keep them alive, the deacons did not mind, and the members (or most of them) welcomed the additional time and leisure which came about as Sunday Schools shrank or closed.

3. Answering Today's Objections

WHAT LINE of reasoning have we devised to relieve ourselves of blame or responsibility for the demise of Sunday Schools? This writer hears at least six arguments being employed to dismiss and disparage Sunday Schooling. The first, already mentioned, is the claim that there is no warrant in the Scripture for child evangelism or Sunday Schools. This claim will be addressed at length in another chapter, for it is the most important (and the most dangerous) of the arguments.

'Sunday Schools are a recent innovation'

Alongside this refusal to see the scriptural warrant is the assertion that Sunday Schools were a late arrival on the unfolding scene of church history. The reasoning runs – 'How can you say that something which only arrived at the end of the eighteenth century can be so crucial, so central and so important?'

This objection altogether misses the point. The instruction of children was always a matter of great concern to the divines of the Reformation and Puritan periods. But those who scorn Sunday Schools as 'late innovations' forget that until the eighteenth century, *all* people in Britain (including children) went to church first by force of law, and then by universal convention, and the very idea of *outreach* to the 'unchurched' was irrelevant. Sunday Schools began in earnest towards the end of the eighteenth century as soon as the Western nations emerged from their long history of church attendance by compulsion and by universal convention.

Indeed, Sunday Schools sprang into being as a very quick response to a new phenomenon – the appearance of the 'apostate' city-poor, with their neglected or discarded ragged children. New converts from the Methodist Awakening were especially instrumental in appealing to this new, non-churchgoing class, and organising its children into Sunday Schools.

It is remarkably unfair to disdain Sunday Schools as a late arrival on the historical scene, when in reality they were an extremely speedy response (in the spirit of the great commission) to a new situation, namely the falling-away from universal churchgoing which followed the great era of the Puritans. Sunday Schools arose to gather in those who, in an earlier generation, needed no gathering.

Sunday Schools arose almost as early as they could have done, catering for a situation which continues to this day – the unreached condition of countless young people. *That* generation of believers took seriously their responsibility to reach out. Do we?

Another argument heard today against the operation of Sunday Schools is the view that the instruction of the young is entirely the responsibility of parents, a curious manner of thinking which limits the scope of the great commission of our Lord to the adult community. Of course we must include children in our evangelistic commission, and especially those children who receive no spiritual help from their parents.

'Sunday Schools never featured in reformation or revival'

Yet another objection to Sunday Schools is expressed in the claim that they have never been conspicuous in the finest seasons of the history of the church, such as in times of awakening and reformation, but this is a line of argument which simply does not stand up to the facts.

It must be remembered that prior to the eighteenth century, when a non-churchgoing underclass appeared for the first time, children's outreach was hardly a relevant concept, for Sunday Schools were already, in effect, built into the churches. What mattered to the Reformers and the Puritans was to teach the Truth to the huge captive audiences to which they ministered.

During those times when everyone went to church (first by law, and then by unbreakable convention), considerable attention was paid to children. Indeed, so important was the religious instruction of children considered, that royal children could frequently read their Greek New Testaments before the age of seven, and catechising was virtually universal throughout Britain.

The great Baptist pastor Benjamin Keach was typical of most Baptists in his attitude to the instruction of children. He was charged in 1664 with 'writing, printing and publishing a schismatical book entitled, *The Child's Instructor or a New and Easy Primer'*. Tried by Chief Justice Hyde, he was heavily fined, summoned to appear at the next assize to recant his doctrines, sentenced to prison for two weeks, and ordered to be pilloried, and to have his book burned. The authorities held that the doctrine of the established church alone should be taught to children.

Then, with the rise of a non-churchgoing class, with its unchurched children, Sunday School outreach became the chosen method of the eighteenth century revival churches to gather in the outcasts. And just as Sunday Schools were born out of revival, so they were to be instrumental in further awakenings.

A great spate of Sunday School openings marked the

rediscovery of the evangelistic spirit by British Baptists when they escaped from a period of hyper-Calvinism at the end of the eighteenth century. These schools contributed greatly to a new golden age of Baptist expansion. The pioneer missionary William Carey, a product of that escape, placed tremendous emphasis on the spiritual nurture of the young in his mighty work in India.

In the United States the Sunday School movement also blossomed and flourished to a remarkable extent, being used of God in the conversion and consolidation of almost entire regions.

There is great significance in the statistic given by the Earl of Shaftesbury, when in 1831 he unveiled a statue of Robert Raikes. He declared that 1¼ million English children were then attending Sunday Schools, a remarkable number bearing in mind the much smaller population of that time.

Just twenty-eight years later, when the Sunday School scholars of 1831 had reached their thirties and early forties, the British Isles were visited again in a wonderful way by the Spirit of God – the 1859 Revival. Sunday Schools, the response of the eighteenth century to a *new* situation, and the fruit of revival, were undoubtedly used by God to prepare the hearts and consciences of the population for the great visitation of the nineteenth century. The only adequate answer to the charge that child evangelism and Sunday Schools have not been conspicuous in times of reformation and revival is to say that it is unhistorical nonsense.

'Sunday Schools have failed to check apostasy'

Other modern protesters against Sunday Schools put the point a little differently, saying, in effect, 'We can prove that Sunday Schools have not been successful by comparing the zenith of the Sunday School movement at the end of the nineteenth century with the general apostasy which took place at the beginning of this century. Sunday Schools, in their season of greatest prosperity, failed to sustain the cause.'

Once again, the charge is wholly mistaken and unfair, being based on a total misreading of history. Moreover, no other form of outreach is expected to endure in effectiveness from generation to generation. We do not blame Puritanism for the Arianism of the next generation; nor the Victorian revivals for the scientific rationalism which followed.

In 1678 Dr Increase Mather, President of Harvard College, Boston, lamented the apostasy of the *second* generation of the New England fathers. For some thirty years their newly founded churches had experienced the continuous breath of awakening, but of their children Mather said:– 'The rising generation is a poor, perishing, unconverted, and . . . an undone generation. Many are profane, drunkards, lascivious, scoffers at the power of godliness . . . others are only civil and outwardly conformed to good order . . . but never knew what the new birth means . . . the glory is departed.'

They, incidentally, did not have Sunday Schools, but they *had* tasted revival during their childhood and adolescence. Do we therefore hear people dismissing revival as ineffective?

But to return to the charge that Sunday Schools, in their finest hour, failed the churches, the unassailable facts show the opposite to be the case. At the beginning of this century, when Darwinism, Higher Criticism, and Modernism began to empty the churches, evangelical Sunday Schools alone slowed the avalanche which threatened.

About ten years ago, an author who was doubtful about Sunday Schools put into print some statistics about Sunday School and church attendance in the district in which the Metropolitan Tabernacle stands. These showed that at the end of the nineteenth century there were wonderful attendances at the various Sunday Schools – well over half the recorded children in the district being found in the churches and chapels for the Sunday School hour. But within a few years only two per cent of working class adults were to be found attending church. On the basis of these figures, the conclusion was drawn that Sunday Schools, even in their heyday, were a failure!

Unfortunately the writer had not properly researched

his figures, taking as his later statistic for working class adult attendance the unsubstantiated generalisation of a cynical (modern) sociologist. In reality, the known attendances of several Bible-believing churches of that time show how well and how long working class attendance held up in the area, *because of the influence of Sunday Schools.* The Metropolitan Tabernacle (which continued to be a congregation largely of working class people) still exceeded 3000 in the early part of this century. Its associated missions all continued in the *high* hundreds, and other evangelical churches accounted together for thousands more.

The fall in adult churchgoing was nothing like as great as irresponsible claims have suggested, and although a steep decline did set in (particularly after the First World War), very large congregations continued to gather – largely because of the immensely effective work of evangelical Sunday Schools.

Since the First World War there have been several outpourings of the Spirit in Britain of both a regional and local kind. Here at the Metropolitan Tabernacle in the 1930s (during the ministry of Harry Tydeman Chilvers), there were several exceptionally fruitful years with many 'surprising conversions'. The area, we remember, was still very blessed with Sunday Schools.

We also read of the ministry of Dr Martyn Lloyd-Jones in South Wales in the 1920s, and of the movement of the Spirit that brought many from darkness to light through his preaching. We marvel that in times of depression and great hardness of heart, the power of God was revealed.

But again, we must note that the consciences of almost all the people, though hard, had once been trained in evangelical Sunday Schools, so that all had some grasp of the standards of God, and some respect for high and holy things. The labours of bygone Sunday School teachers had not been in vain, nor did they go unrewarded.

Today, the mission field of Britain has a very different appearance. There is little of fields which are *white already to harvest*, but there are acres of thorns, briars and scrub. The loss of Sunday Schools has left a scene of spiritual devastation – an utterly heathen land. A new generation of preachers no longer assumes responsibility for communities trained in Sunday Schools. The Lord's servants now conduct their ministries surrounded by total atheism. When they visit a street, hardly anyone now says, 'Yes, I used to go to Sunday School.' Scarcely anyone knows anything about the strange and alien faith they represent.

The writer with a small band of helpers was involved about thirty years ago in the pioneering of a church in a new town in South Hertfordshire. The nucleus of that new cause came from the ingathering of people who had been instructed in Sunday Schools in Central London in pre-war years. They were the people who were most readily brought under the sound of the Word, their consciences rekindled after so many years. But where is their equivalent today?

Today's church planters and preachers have vastly more to do than their predecessors for two centuries – due to the loss of Sunday Schools! And what kind of situation will we pass on to our successors, if the Lord delays His coming? *We* inherited a harvest field served by tiny Sunday Schools. Our successors, in so many towns and villages, will labour where for many years there will have been none at all.

Sunday Schools were certainly not a failure in their heyday, and those who claim that they were show a startling unfamiliarity with the spiritual history of both Britain and America. It would be a sad matter if believers were influenced by a claim so absurdly forced and unworthy of debate.

'Sunday Schools are no longer effective'

Some opponents of Sunday Schools take a slightly more conciliatory line saying, 'This is all very well; Sunday Schools have undoubtedly done a good job in the past, but they are entirely inappropriate for the present day. They have had their day. The fact is that children can no longer be gathered on the scale once possible. In spiritual terms they are no longer cost-effective. They take an enormous amount of work for a very small reward. The children just will not come, and therefore we must face up to a changed situation.'

We simply must challenge this line of reasoning also. Would friends apply the same reasoning to adult Sunday services? Would they abandon them also, because congregations cannot be gathered on the scale of the past?

Cynicism about the Sunday School's effectiveness, however, is entirely misguided. The fact is that large Sunday Schools may still be gathered where the people of God have a heart and a will to *work*! The only limitations will usually be space and staffing.

The problem is not that the children cannot be gathered. This writer hears keen Sunday School workers complaining that in their church the pastor shows no interest and gives no support. Nor can church members be prevailed upon to lend a hand as teachers or as 'transporters'.

It has been proved repeatedly that Sunday Schools – in most areas – are still a most successful agency for gathering young people under the Word, and that any experience to the contrary is usually due to the fact that the church makes only a feeble, token effort, and leaves the work to a tiny band of people.

If only the hearts of the people of God could be moved to long again for the youth and children of the land to hear the Word of God and live! If only those of us who are pastors and office-bearers could be persuaded to reassume a burden of responsibility for the spiritual and moral training of *all* the young people in our towns and neighbourhoods!

If only we could learn to identify more with that profound revelation of the heart of God uttered by the Saviour – *Even so it is not the will of your Father which is in heaven, that one of these little ones should perish!*

4. The Biblical Warrant for the Evangelisation of all Children

BIBLE-BELIEVING CHRISTIANS do not need to apologise for Sunday Schools. God's revealed will is that *the earth shall be filled with the knowledge of the glory of the Lord, as the waters cover the sea;* and the church's duty is to use all means at her disposal to bring that about. In fact, the great end for which she exists – subordinate only to the glorifying of God – is the evangelisation of all people in this world.

Clearly, that necessitates bringing the Gospel to children; and so, in both Testaments, God calls His people to this work. In this chapter I want to show the biblical warrant for reaching children and establishing Sunday Schools.

OLD TESTAMENT TEACHING

Here are ten Old Testament arguments in support of Sunday Schools. Afterwards I will give arguments from the New Testament.

1. The example of Adam and the Patriarchs

First, in the book of *Genesis,* we discover that Adam was the first teacher of children, and a very remarkable teacher he was. He taught all the children in the world! *Genesis 4* records how his two sons, Cain and Abel, brought offerings to the Lord their God. But who told them when, where, and how to approach their Maker? Adam! We are told that Abel offered his sacrifice *by faith (Hebrews 11.4),* and since faith comes by *the word of God (Romans 10.17),* we conclude that Adam instructed these children in the doctrines and precepts of true religion.

The patriarchs followed him in this, and the evidence shows that they taught not only their own children but also the children of their servants. Concerning Abraham, for example, God says, *I know him, that he will command his children and his household after him, and they shall keep the way of the Lord, to do justice and judgment (Genesis 18.19).*

I believe Abraham took his responsibility seriously. At any rate, *Genesis 14.14* refers to *his trained servants* or, as the margin renders it, 'his instructed servants', meaning those whom he had taught. Jacob did the same. We read how he spoke to *his household, and to all that were with him,* exhorting them to repentance and to reconsecration. *Put away the strange gods that are among you,* he said, *and be clean, and change your garments: and let us arise, and go up to Bethel (Genesis 35.2-3). All that were with him* would have included friends, servants, proselytes – *and* children. Patriarchal religion certainly involved the teaching of children; and, when this duty was performed, God approved of it. For this reason, if for no other, it receives honourable mention in His Word.

2. The duty of care for little ones

Secondly, we read that God impressed upon the Israelites the need to show spiritual care for *little ones.* That is an expression which occurs time and time again in the early books of the Old Testament. Some of these references show that God Himself is deeply concerned about the well-being of *little ones.*

He is reported as saying in *Numbers 14.31, your little ones . . . will I bring in, and they shall know the land which ye have despised.* But He would have His people share that concern too. At the ceremony of covenant renewal, He required Israel's leaders to call the people together – *men, and women, and* CHILDREN, *and thy stranger that is within thy gates . . .* [in order] *that their children, which have not known any thing may hear, and*

37

learn to fear the Lord your God (Deuteronomy 31.12-13).

Commenting upon those words, Professor Ridderbos says, 'All these must thus learn to fear the Lord and to keep this law. Verse 13 states the same thing specifically with regard to the children (who were also included in v12; cf 4.9; 11.19); it is especially necessary for them because they, unlike their parents, have not yet been instructed in the law.' (Compare similar references in *Exodus 10.10; 12.26-27; Deuteronomy 4.9; 11.19; Joshua 4.6-7.*)

According to Mosaic law, God does have something to say to children, and that is why they need to be assembled. He says, *thou shalt teach them* [ie: the commandments] *diligently unto thy children (Deuteronomy 6.7).* In the original, it is 'unto thy sons', and the Jews have always understood that to mean, not only natural sons, but also young disciples or scholars, because elsewhere in Scripture 'teachers' are referred to as 'fathers', and 'pupils' as 'sons' *(2 Kings 2.12; 4.1).* Thus understood, this is a clear command to teach the Word to children.

3. Youth is biblically the best time to teach

Thirdly, we find emphasis being placed upon the time of youth as the very best time to be instructed. God, for example, tells how He loved and trained Israel when Israel was but a child: that is, in the very earliest stages of national existence. *When Israel was a child, then I loved him . . . I taught Ephraim also to go, taking them by their arms (Hosea 11.1, 3).* His dealing with the nation in the time of its childhood provides an example for us. We too should seize the opportunity of that period, making every effort to lead young people into the way of everlasting life.

Another scripture enabling us to make the same application is *Jeremiah 2.2.* There, God says, *I remember thee, the kindness of thy youth.* He is looking back again to the early days, to Israel's first love. How pleasing it was to Him! I suggest there is something very wrong with us if we find no delight in the praises of little children, their calling upon the Saviour's name, and their attentiveness to the plan of redemption. If our hearts were *anything* like His, we would truly rejoice in these things.

The point being made is underlined for us in the ceremonial law, where God specifically requires the *first-fruits,* as He does, for example, in *Leviticus 2.14: If thou offer a meat offering of thy firstfruits unto the Lord, thou shalt offer for the meat offering of thy firstfruits green ears of corn dried by the fire, even corn beaten out of full ears.* Thomas Manton sees here an important principle and comments as follows: 'God would not stay till [it] ripened. God will not be long kept out of His portion. *Youth is our best time.*'

In other words, Manton understands from these ritual laws that God wants the young, the fresh, and the tender; and his observation leads him to conclude, quite rightly, that God wants young people.

Further proof of this may be found in the fact that God Himself is prepared to teach them. The psalmist bears witness to this, saying, *Thou hast taught me from my youth (Psalm 71.17)*. It surely follows that we too should teach them – and in a suitable way, as Scripture itself suggests.

When the people of Judah criticised Isaiah for treating them like children, like *them that are weaned from the milk, and drawn from the breasts,* they complained that the prophet acted towards them like a schoolteacher, using basic and repetitive instruction. *For precept must be upon precept, precept upon precept; line upon line, line upon line; here a little, and there a little (Isaiah 28.9-10)*. Although this is the language of contempt, these words do make clear that children need a special kind of teaching – the simplest possible.

4. Specialised tutors were sanctioned

Fourthly, while it certainly was a duty incumbent upon parents to instruct their children *(Proverbs 4.3-4; 31.1),* others were by no means excluded from this ministry: hence the reference in *1 Chronicles 25.8* to *teacher* and *scholar.* I realise that this is in the context of musical service, and that it primarily relates to the art of singing, but commentators tell us that it is proverbial in form, suggesting that the relation of teacher and scholar was a familiar one at that time. Note the reference in *2 Kings 10.1* and *5* to *the bringers up of the children,* and also the fact that, according to *Daniel 1.11,* a man called Melzar was tutor to young Daniel.

A closer look at the Old Testament will reveal that there were guilds of recognised scribes or wise men – *the families of the scribes (1 Chronicles 2.55).* These were responsible for teaching the Word of God to Israel's children; and apparently David was one of those who benefited from their teaching. *Psalm 119.99* finds him saying, *I have more understanding than all my teachers: for thy testimonies are my meditation.* I concur with the view of Dr Barnes who believes that David is probably referring here to 'those who had given him instruction in early life'.

5. A book of child instruction was provided

Fifthly, the book of *Proverbs* may justly be called 'the oldest handbook on education'. Archbishop Perowne says of it, 'In the book of Proverbs, the wise teacher of the young, propounding to his children as they sit around his feet, maxims of guidance and warning in the untried path of life before them, gives them this as the keynote, the root, the motto of all his teaching, *The fear of Jehovah is the beginning of knowledge.'*

Throughout this book, the teacher assumes a fatherly relation. *My son,* he says, *hear the instruction of thy father (Proverbs 1.8,* cf *1.10, 15; 2.1; 3.1, 11).* But recall

41

what has been earlier stated, namely that in Israel 'teachers' were regarded as 'fathers'. When Saul was called to be king, for example, the people said, *Is Saul also among the prophets? . . . Who is their father? (1 Samuel 10.11-12.)* By that second question they meant, 'Who is the teacher of these young men?' The answer, of course, was Samuel.

Returning now to *Proverbs*, when we read the word 'father', we are not so much to think of a natural father (although it can have that application), but we are rather to think of one in the teaching office gathering children around him in order to teach them the Word of God. *Hear me now therefore, O ye children, and depart not from the words of my mouth . . . Lest . . . thou mourn at the last . . . and say, How have I hated instruction, and my heart despised reproof; and have not obeyed the voice of MY TEACHERS, nor inclined mine ear to THEM THAT INSTRUCTED ME! (Proverbs 5.7-13.)*

In passing, take note of the fact that *The Larger Catechism* identifies the 'father and mother' of the fifth commandment as, not only natural parents, but also 'all superiors in age, gifts, and especially such as, by God's ordinance, are over us in place of authority, whether in family, church, or commonwealth.'

So then, if someone asks what biblical warrant you have for teaching children in Sunday Schools, just tell them to read the book of *Proverbs*!

6. The priests taught children

Sixthly, Old Testament ministers took special interest in the teaching of young people. Take the case of Jehoiada. He undertook to teach the crown prince, Jehoash, who came to the throne when only seven years old. *Jehoash,* we read, *did that which was right in the sight of the Lord all his days wherein Jehoiada the priest instructed him (2 Kings 12.2).*

What an interesting verse that is! It declares how a teaching priest undertook the religious education of a child in order that he might bring him up in the fear of the Lord. The question George Barlow asks in *The Homiletic Commentary,* is, 'What would have become of Jehoash if he had been brought up at the court of his idolatrous father and his depraved mother?' He adds, 'God gave him in Jehoiada far more than he had lost in his father and mother.'

It is all very well for some reformed ministers to say, 'Parents are responsible for teaching their children and we therefore reject the whole concept of Sunday Schools.' What if the parents are ungodly, as is (sadly) the case with the majority today? Do we stand by and allow an entire generation of children to perish? God forbid! May the Lord raise up from among us men and women like Jehoiada who will be willing to take the parents' place and teach the Truth to children.

7. Special children's assemblies

Seventhly, there are verses which speak of the assembling of children for this very purpose. *Joel 2.16* is one such verse: *Gather the children. Psalm 34.11* is another: *Come, ye children, hearken unto me: I will teach you the fear of the Lord.*

In the former verse, the children were summoned along with all the people to a solemn assembly; in the latter, they were called to a meeting especially convened for them. We certainly do believe that children should be encouraged to attend ordinary church services *(Deuteronomy 29.11; Ezra 10.1)*, but we also believe that a biblical case can be made out for special children's meetings.

The church is told in *Song of Solomon 1.8 – Feed thy kids beside the shepherds'* [or pastors'] *tents*. If you consult the Jewish commentators, you will discover that they understand by *tents*, religious schools. It is an interesting interpretation, worthy of further thought. But whether we accept it or not, one thing is very clear: the church *must* take spiritual care of young children.

Implied here, too, is the fact that the young, like *kids*, have their own way of feeding. A supporting scripture would be *Isaiah 5.17 – Then shall the lambs feed AFTER THEIR MANNER*. A literal rendering of the Hebrew would be 'according to their grazing', and the thought is that lambs feed in their own way – usually together, with evident joy, and on tender grass. The point is: children do the same, and for that very reason we need Sunday Schools.

8. God promises to bless children

Eighthly, there are many passages in the prophets which intimate God's willingness to bless children. One says, *I will pour my spirit upon thy seed, and my blessing upon thine offspring (Isaiah 44.3)*. Another declares, *All thy children shall be taught of the Lord (Isaiah 54.13)*. What encouragement this is to those who teach the young!

A study of sacred history will reveal that many people were converted in childhood. We think at once of the child Samuel whom the Lord called *(1 Samuel 3.1, 4)*. David too comes to mind, because he could say, *Thou art my hope, O Lord God: thou art my trust from my youth (Psalm 71.5)*.

Then there is Abijah, Jeroboam's son, in whom, Scripture says, there was found *some good thing toward the Lord God of Israel (1 Kings 14.13)*. Obadiah is another fine example. He once told the prophet Elijah, *I thy servant fear the Lord from my youth (1 Kings 18.12)*. And, of course, we cannot omit mention of Josiah, the boy king, who *while he was yet young . . . began to seek after the God of David his father (2 Chronicles 34.3)*.

Why is it that we are given so many examples of believing children? It is surely to show us how important and profitable it is to teach them. Quaint old Philip Henry (father of Matthew) used to say, 'A young saint, an old angel'. He observed that Obadiah, who feared the Lord from his youth, is said to have *feared the Lord greatly (1 Kings 18.3)*, and 'those that would come to fear God *greatly*,' he would say, 'must learn to fear Him *from their youth*.' But how shall they fear Him if they are left without the knowledge of God?

9. Childhood and youth are especially for the Lord

Ninthly, the Jews recognised youth as a momentous time when decisions are made affecting eternity. Solomon does not hesitate to speak directly to children, saying, *Remember* NOW *thy Creator* IN THE DAYS OF THY YOUTH *(Ecclesiastes 12.1)*. Why remember Him in the days of youth?

In the first place, because God deserves the very best time of our lives.

Secondly, because it will avoid the futile, painful search for happiness among the things of this world.

Thirdly, it will prevent the heart from being hardened by continuance in sin.

Fourthly, the Lord may cease to call, His Spirit may cease to strive, and we shall then be given over to a reprobate mind.

Fifthly, evil days will surely come, and after them, death itself when it will be for ever too late.

Sixthly, the uncertainty of life means that none can be sure of a tomorrow, nor even of one further opportunity to repent and believe.

And seventhly – perhaps the most important truth to be grasped – the way a person chooses in youth often determines where he will spend eternity.

Along with such commands, there are most encouraging promises. The Lord says, *I love them that love me; and those that seek me early shall find me (Proverbs 8.17).* Bring in the children, tell them of God's salvation, call them to believe with all their hearts on the Lord Jesus Christ. And Sunday School teachers, you have God's Word for it: you will *not* labour in vain.

10. The example of synagogue schools

Tenthly, and lastly, mention should be made of the synagogue schools. We do not hesitate to maintain that the synagogue was of divine institution, even though, as in the case of sacrifice, the original appointment is not recorded. In the Mosaic arrangements, room was made for it in such words as *Leviticus 23.3, Six days shall work be done: but the seventh day is the sabbath of rest, an holy convocation* (cf *Psalm 74.8*).

From the Talmud we learn that synagogues have long had their schools for children. Campegius Vitringa, a recognised authority on the subject, informs us that these schools were invariably in the same building as the synagogue, and, in sparsely populated areas, the same room answered for the twofold purpose of divine worship and religious instruction. Since the Christian church was modelled after the synagogue (see *James 2.2* margin), this fact obviously has considerable relevance and significance.

Contrary to some people's opinion, the Old Testament has a great deal to say about the teaching of children. Its teaching is plain, and there is no need to quote obscure texts, strain the meaning of words, or indulge in dubious exegesis.

NEW TESTAMENT TEACHING

Perhaps the first thing we should learn from the New Testament is that, as a child, our Lord was prepared to be taught the truth of the Scriptures. *They found him . . . in the midst of the doctors, both hearing them, and asking them questions (Luke 2.46).* This was within the precincts of the Temple, probably in a synagogue where rabbis taught the Word of God to children. So we have here, as Bishop Wordsworth observes, 'The Child Jesus submitting to be catechised by the authorised teachers of God's law in God's house.'

And as an old Latin saying states, 'Omnis Christi actio nostra instructio' or 'Every action of Christ is our instruction.' Children are hereby taught to come to the house of God for Christian instruction.

During His public ministry, our Lord showed a particular interest in children. Had we the space, it would be profitable to consider in detail some of the beautiful Gospel passages which describe His contacts with them (eg: *Matthew 14.21; 15.38; 18.3; 19.13-14; 21.15-16*). These passages led Dr Steel to say, 'He became incarnate in a baby, and Himself passed through all the stages of infancy and youth to the manhood which He reached. He had a fellow-feeling for them.'

On one notable occasion, He said, *Suffer little children, and forbid them not, to come unto me: for of such is the kingdom of heaven (Matthew 19.14).* Who were the children He had in mind? Not infants, it seems, but little boys and girls, because He called them to Him and they were quite capable of coming to Him by themselves.

The Greek word used for *little children* is applied in another place to a child about twelve years old (*Mark 5.39, 42 – the damsel,* or rather 'the little child'). The Lord Jesus loved to gather the children in order to bless them. Would that Christians showed more of His spirit!

As *a prophet mighty in deed* as well as *word,* there must surely be significance in the fact that our Lord performed some of His miracles on children. We think of Jairus's daughter, the daughter of the Syro-Phoenician woman, and that child who was tragically vexed by the devil *(Matthew 9, 15* and *17).* Of the last case, we read, *the child was cured from that very hour.*

Is this just a story? No, like all the miracles, it was a *sign,* a symbol or emblem of Christ's working in the sphere of grace and in the spiritual domain. It illustrated the love which is at the centre of the Gospel and shows that part of our Saviour's mission was to bring that love to bear upon the needs of the young.

As always, Mr Spurgeon has a pertinent remark to make. 'There was,' he says, 'no need for the boy to wait till he grew up. He was under the power of the devil while he was a child, and he was cured as a child. Let us seek the salvation of children as children.'

One all-important reason why we should do so is the fact that children can be converted. Christ believed that. He taught that it was possible for a child savingly to believe on His name. *Whoso shall receive one such . . . child . . . receiveth me. But whoso shall offend one of these* LITTLE ONES WHICH BELIEVE IN ME, *it were better for him that a millstone were hanged about his neck, and that he were drowned in the depth of the sea (Matthew 18.5-6).*

On the basis of that scripture, I have this to say to our critics: *How shall they believe in him of whom they have not heard? and how shall they hear without a preacher? (Romans 10.14.)*

Reference was earlier made to Mr Spurgeon. In 1866, a conference was held in the Metropolitan Tabernacle, presided over by Mr Spurgeon, and in one of the addresses, entitled *The Importance of Seeking the Conversion of the Young*, the speaker alluded to 'the many little ones who had true faith in Christ in the days of His flesh'. He then went on to say, 'No part of our population is of equal importance with the juvenile portion of it, and I believe that among none beside will the same amount of earnest, prayerful, loving labour meet with a larger, or even an equal measure of success.' If nothing else does, that at least should motivate and stir us into action. But there is more to be said.

It is God's will that we reach and teach children. The Lord Jesus said, *Take heed that ye despise not one of these little ones; for I say unto you, That in heaven their angels do always behold the face of my Father which is in heaven (Matthew 18.10)*. Can you see the point He is making? God has entrusted angels with the special care of children; and if God's will is ever to be done on earth as it is in Heaven, Christians must feel a like responsibility for them, doing all they can to secure the safety and well-being of their souls. We read about their *angels*, but where today are their *teachers*?

Is this care included in the church's commission? Yes, it is. The Lord assigned to Peter (and therefore to disciples in every age) the care of children when He said, *Feed my lambs (John 21.15)*. Dr Richard Lenski brings out the meaning when he says, 'Jesus mentions the lambs first, but certainly not because they are less valuable or require less care; rather the reverse is true . . . Jesus here places His most loved possessions into Peter's care. The spiritual feeding and nourishment of children is here made the first part of the great apostolic office.' It goes without saying that Christ's words, while originally spoken to Peter, are actually addressed to all believers. This being the church's duty, it explains the repeated occurrence in the New Testament of the word 'catechise' *(Luke 1.4; Acts 18.25; Galatians 6.6)*. The word literally means 'to sound down [the ears]': thus, 'to teach by word of mouth'. However, from earliest times it has been employed in a more restricted sense to denote elementary instruction of the young by way of questions and answers.

Well might we lament with Thomas Manton the lack of catechising among us! 'For want of this pattern of sound words, and these condescensions to weak ones by this exercise, many mischiefs have abounded amongst us, to the great damage of religion and godliness.'

As the apostle reminds us, We are debtors *both to the wise, and to the unwise (Romans 1.14)*. We are therefore under obligation to convey the knowledge of the Truth both to adults and to children. Yet, as we learned from the Old Testament, the Truth has to be dispensed according to children's capacities.

This is the principle taught in *Hebrews 5.12* which mentions *such as have need of milk, and not of strong meat*. The church which provides only adult sermons for young people may think it is being faithful, but in actual fact it is far from the right path. Children require teaching adapted to their particular needs.

When Christ's church took seriously the matter of reaching and teaching children, it enjoyed great favour and remarkable prosperity. If, once again, we were to take it seriously, who can tell what God might do? Listen to the Elizabethan preacher, Lancelot Andrewes: 'What effect the Apostles' and their followers' catechising had, Hegesippus testifies, saying that hereby it came to pass that no known commonwealth in that part of the world was inhabited which within forty years after Christ's passion felt not a great shaking of its heathenish superstition. Julian the Apostate, the grand and subtle enemy of Christianity, perceiving this, inhibited and suppressed all Christian schools.'

What then should we do? We should be filled with a desire and resolve to establish Sunday Schools in our churches. And if one is already established, we should determine to engage all our powers for its enlargement.

In the Scottish Assembly of 1796, Hamilton, a leading Moderate, delivered an eloquent speech against foreign missions. 'To spread abroad the knowledge of the gospel among barbarous and heathen nations,' he said, 'seems to me to be highly preposterous . . . Let us unite in resolutely rejecting these overtures.'

At length he finished speaking, and sat down. Immediately, Dr John Erskine, the venerable leader of the evangelical party, rose to his feet and pointing to the Bible on the table of the General Assembly, he uttered the memorable words, 'Moderator, rax me that Bible.'

With the open Bible in his hand, Dr Erskine then proceeded to refute all Hamilton's arguments, conclusively establishing the scriptural case for the evangelisation of the heathen.

Some in our day (who should know better) are vocal in their opposition to Sunday Schools. For our part, we would stand with Erskine; and if any question our warrant, we shall simply point to God's holy Book, and say, 'Reach me that Bible!'

5. Five Binding Principles

THE BIBLICAL IMPERATIVE for the evangelisation of children is so clear that it may be approached from many scriptural passages and principles. Here are a further five fundamental principles, each of which demands Sunday School outreach in our day, and shapes the way we should go about it.

1. God's character requires child evangelism

The first principle is simple yet overwhelmingly powerful – the revealed *character* of Almighty God demands such a ministry. We see this in those glorious words – *Even so it is not the will of your Father which is in heaven, that one of these little ones should perish.* We should particularly note the word *Father*.

We are taught in *Genesis 1.26* that we are made in

God's image. Clearly, those who worship and adore Almighty God will especially value and seek to exercise those faculties and inclinations which reflect His divine being.

Almighty God is a personal and relational being, and we too are *personal, relational* beings. Accordingly, in the church, *God setteth the solitary in families (Psalm 68.6),* and calls His people to *love one another,* and express Christian fellowship. God is infinitely intelligent, and we, being in His image, are *rational* beings, possessing the gift of reason. We are repeatedly commanded to value and exercise this priceless faculty. The Lord says – *Be not children in understanding . . . but in understanding be men (1 Corinthians 14.20).*

Although the image of God is tarnished and obscured in us, we still reflect Him as *moral* beings, possessing a moral conscience, which we are commanded to heed, hold and keep pure *(1 Timothy 1.19 and 3.9).* In every respect that we are bearers of the divine image, we are to treasure that endowment, and exercise it with diligence and fervour.

The particular attribute of God – reflected in us – which bears on child evangelism is His wonderful *fatherliness.* God is a Father, and He is presented in the Scriptures as *a father of the fatherless (Psalm 68.5).* He is especially fatherly towards disadvantaged children. Made in the image of God, we bear the same parental instinct and concern, not only for our children, but in some measure for all children, and especially the disadvantaged. Even unregenerate people give evidence of being made in the image of a heavenly *Father*, for however tarnished that image may be, they usually possess a strong compassion for children.

Note how concerned worldlings are, generally speaking, to love, cherish, care for and guide children. It is natural because, as image-bearers, God has fixed His likeness in us. Even the ungodly are concerned to rescue the children first in circumstances of danger. Even the unsaved world is concerned for the education and protection of children.

Supremely, though, this concern has always been seen in the hearts of believers. We think of George Muller, Dr Tom Barnardo and C. H. Spurgeon with their great homes for destitute boys and girls, and we see how in the past the hearts of such Christian people (the image of God reactivated in them) have been touched by the plight of the underprivileged.

Our supreme adoration of God's character, together with the desire to express the fatherly image which we bear, leads us to be concerned for children, and especially for those in greatest spiritual deprivation. The basis of child evangelism or Sunday School outreach is nothing less than the wonderful fatherliness of our God, and the influence of the image stamped upon our own beings.

If we have no heart for the rising generation, we deny

our privileged status as image-bearers, and show contempt for the very heart of God. If we have no concern for spiritually destitute children, we must think of what this means!

Can it be that Bible-believing churches should deny and suppress the very image of God upon them? Can it be that we should wilfully suppress and deny our God-given instinct to care for spiritual orphans? Can it be that we should grow so cold as to lose our desire to bring glory to God in the hearts of the young?

It is, of course, unthinkable that an enlightened worshipper of the Father should ever disparage or oppose child evangelism. Yet, extraordinary though it may seem, it has become necessary in our day to rearticulate the biblical warrant for work among the young. This is not a cause with a 'weak case', for which we must take a defensive stance. It is a cause for which every true Christian should possess a strong, instinctual desire and commitment – arising from the fatherliness of God planted in every heart.

2. The commission is comprehensive

A second principle, which virtually insists on Sunday Schools for our times stems from the great commission of our Lord, which commands the church to evangelise all nations, including *every* creature.* The vital principle

---

*Matthew 28.19-20 and Mark 16.15.

here is the *universality of the great commission*. The command to preach the Gospel to every creature is universal, which means that the Gospel must be preached (as far as God enables us) to *all* people in the world, and to *all kinds* of people in *all kinds* of conditions. The great commission directs us to all nations, all age groups, and, literally, as many individuals as we can possibly reach.

In the great commission the Lord does not say to pastors, 'Try to reach a reasonable number in your community. As long as you are modestly busy in the work of the Gospel, you will be discharging your responsibility.' He says – preach to *every* creature. We are to be stretching for all we are worth to reach as many people as possible. Amazingly, there are friends today – even in the ministry – who seem to doubt the universality of the great commission!

This principle obviously bears on the matter of Sunday Schools and their desirability. Do they open up for us a fresh and effective opportunity of ministry to an unreached sector of the community? If so, then the great commission effectively *commands* them.

Look at the success of the early church, portrayed by Luke in *Acts 5.28*. Here Luke records the charge made against the apostles by the high priest:– *Did not we straitly command you that ye should not teach in this name? and, behold, ye have filled Jerusalem with your doctrine, and intend to bring this man's blood upon us.*

This verse provides a precious insight into *how* the apostles obeyed the great commission. They aimed at nothing less than *filling the city* with the knowledge of their message! What a difference between their work and ours! In *Acts 5.42* we see how the first Christians achieved their target:– *Daily in the temple, and in every house, they ceased not to teach and preach Jesus Christ.*

The warrant and the command for evangelistic neighbourhood Sunday Schools is the universal force of the great commission. We are commanded to *fill* our 'city' with knowledge, and not to ignore sections of the community which may easily be reached, such as the young.

We have, logically, only one possible justification for not attempting Sunday Schools. Is the rising generation of our time being effectively reached by some *other* agency or mechanism? This alone would excuse us from taking advantage of the wonderful opportunities afforded by Sunday Schools. If the young are not being reached, then we *must* operate a vigorous and *evangelistic* Sunday School, or else we are refusing to take seriously the Lord of the great commission. The *universality* of the great commission demands child evangelism.

3. The duty of seizing every opportunity

A third principle which also presses us to evangelistic Sunday Schools is the special and binding duty given to us in the Scripture to *seize every legitimate opportunity* that is presented to us to promote the Gospel effectively. This is a vital guiding principle for us.

Notice the holy opportunism of the apostle Paul. Notice how he sought to grasp significant opportunities to reach the greatest number of people. Luke tells us in *Acts 20.16* that – *Paul had determined to sail by Ephesus, because he would not spend the time in Asia: for he hasted, if it were possible for him, to be at Jerusalem the day of Pentecost.*

Here Paul took as a primary rule of guidance the need to take advantage of a special evangelistic opportunity, in this case the outreach to the greatly swollen population of Jerusalem at the time of Pentecost. The great desirability (and pleasure) of a visit to all his dear friends and converts at Ephesus had to give way to this painful but golden opportunity to reach Jerusalem before the crowds subsided.

Did anyone say to Paul: 'But Paul, what is your specific biblical warrant for bypassing Ephesus to go to Jerusalem?' The apostle gave us – by his example – the principle of godly opportunism. On no account must we despise the duty of special opportunity. It is an apostolic practice to recognise and take seriously both occasions and sections of society which present a special opportunity.

The greatest declaration of this principle is to be found in our Lord's training of the disciples. The sending out of the twelve and then the seventy disciples *(Luke 9* and *10)* includes commands to focus special attention on people who will listen, and not to waste too much time on those who are obdurate.

Of the sending of the twelve, we read:– *Whatsoever house ye enter into, there abide, and thence depart. And whosoever will not receive you, when ye go out of that city, shake off the very dust from your feet for a testimony against them.*

Concerning the sending of the seventy, Luke says:– *After these things the Lord appointed other seventy also, and sent them two and two before his face into every city and place, whither he himself would come. Therefore said he unto them . . . Into whatsoever city ye enter, and they receive you, eat such things as are set before you: and heal the sick that are therein, and say unto them, The kingdom of God is come nigh unto you. But into whatsoever city ye enter, and they receive you not, go your ways out into the streets of the same, and say, Even the very dust of your city, which cleaveth on us, we do wipe off against you: notwithstanding be ye sure of this, that the kingdom of God is come nigh unto you.*

It is true that these were very specialised ministries, but the method laid down by the Lord of concentrating most attention on those cities or towns which would listen, must surely constitute a hallowed ongoing principle. Wherever we are given a special opportunity or hearing, and wherever we may gain ready access, *there* we must concentrate our ministry. Opportunities for a credible hearing must be seized. People who are inclined to hear must never be neglected.

Wherever we are rejected (after serious effort has been made) we must not persist *at the expense of others who may be more open to our word.* There comes a time when the ministry of *grace* must turn into a ministry of *warning*, and then we must go on our way because we have multitudes of other people to reach. That is the principle of the Lord, and on the basis of that principle, we must give particular attention to any city, town or village where we are given a good reception.

This principle clearly transcends town boundaries. It applies not only to places, such as homes, but also to the various strata of society – including age groups. And there is no doubt that we receive an excellent reception today from the young. They are the easiest group to gather, and we must consider the implications of this very carefully, for we are to use the methods laid down by the Lord.

Of course we must gather adults with all our strength. But we would be blind not to recognise that we have unique and special opportunities among the young. Even godless parents are usually eager to commit their children to us for Sunday School, even if only to secure for themselves a quiet hour. It is possible in most towns to gather the young in very great numbers, if we only try. Here is a great part of the town – a generation stratum – that will come and listen, and by the principle taught in the finest seminary that ever existed (our Lord's school for disciples) we have an obligation to take this opportunity.

The point can be illustrated easily from the attendance of Bible-believing churches in our land today. There are many churches which gather about sixty adult hearers to services. These are days of decline, and faithful labourers toil hard to get as many as sixty. Of the sixty, perhaps about fifteen are unconverted. In other words, an evangelistic sermon will be preached to some fifteen hearers.

But let us compare this figure with the possibilities offered by a Sunday School. Most churches with sixty hearers, in a community of reasonable size, could gather a hundred unconverted children relatively easily. It may take a little time, but experience shows that it may be accomplished.

The mathematics should seal the argument. To a total of fifteen unconverted hearers we have the opportunity (through a Sunday School) of adding another hundred. Is this not therefore a unique and special opportunity? Are we not offered by the young a better response and a more sympathetic hearing? Surely, by the Lord's principle an obligation rests upon us to focus effort on the young! A warrant for child evangelism is present in the commands of Christ to the twelve and to the seventy.

We need to challenge our complacency about such

possibilities. What if this special opportunity for Sunday School outreach were to pass? What if British believers were to lose the opportunities provided by the legal protection of the Lord's Day, giving rise to widespread Sunday entertainments and shopping? What if the character of the Lord's Day entirely changed so that it became the same as Saturday, or worse? How would we account before the Lord for the fact that we never attempted to reach the children in all the years of opportunity? Pastors and elders would have to give account, for they have the high duty of steering and inspiring the people of God.

What would we say in our defence if charged with indifference to the Lord's great commission, and its implications for child evangelism? How would we explain ourselves if we have encouraged complacency, and disdained glorious opportunities?

At the present time the United Kingdom still enjoys great privileges and opportunities through the Lord's Day. May it prove to be the case that the sovereign God has determined yet another period of wonderful blessing in the gathering of a new harvest. May churches seize hold of the extraordinary access they have to the young, while there is time.

4. The duty of speaking to every level of understanding

There is yet another principle drawn from the Word

which provides a warrant and a foundation for the ministry of evangelistic Sunday Schools, and it is this:– God requires us to shape and adapt our presentation of Truth to the level of understanding of *all kinds of lost people*. We are to strive to 'match' our ministry, including our language, to people in every human condition.

The key text for this principle is the well-known passage in *1 Corinthians 9.19-22 – For though I be free from all men, yet have I made myself servant unto all, that I might gain the more. And unto the Jews I became as a Jew, that I might gain the Jews; to them that are under the law, as under the law, that I might gain them that are under the law; to them that are without law, as without law . . .*

Of course, the apostle did not adapt to unsaved hearers by behaving in a lawless way. He did not adopt godless customs or godless culture in order to reach people. But he always adapted his approach so as to *be understandable* to all grades of hearer.

When addressing Gentiles, for example, he did not rain texts upon their heads, nor did he use Jewish religious jargon and terminology. He says – *To the weak became I as weak, that I might gain the weak*. Who are the *weak*? They are the strengthless or feeble in any sense (although bodily sickness is clearly not in mind in this passage). Here Paul is thinking of the *ethically* weak, who need specially tailored explanations of the sinfulness of sin and the way of salvation. The principle of *special consideration* for the hearer applies particularly to the largest category of weakness of understanding – the category of children. The principle of the apostle insists on special instruction for them. The apostle who said, *Be ye therefore followers of me,* provides an example of how we should adapt our teaching to the limitations, weaknesses and special needs of hearers.

Today, alas, there is an almost superstitious idea abroad in the churches that if the children are made to sit through adult sermons, God will be especially pleased, and some spiritual benefit will wash off on them whether they understand anything or not. But this was never the apostle's way. He advocated a special approach to each disadvantaged group, and this is the principle which we are bound to adopt.

In *Galatians 4.1-2* the apostle accepts as correct that the children need *tutors and governors* to be prepared for adult life. It is only in present-day evangelical churches that some people seem to think that children need no specialised spiritual instruction.

In *1 Corinthians 3.2* Paul speaks of having a special teaching syllabus for those who are young in spiritual things. He declares: *I have fed you with milk, and not with meat: for hitherto ye were not able to bear it, neither yet now are ye able.* If the apostolic method distinguished between the different capacities of adults, how much more should we distinguish between adults and children.

Paul's grading of instruction is seen again in *1 Corinthians 2.6*, where he says – *Howbeit we speak wisdom among them that are perfect. Hebrews 5.11-14* is another passage in which 'babes' must be instructed in a special way.

The *principle* to be honoured today is that multitudes of lost children must be reached through an outreach ministry which presents the Gospel in a language and with reasoning which *they* can follow *and* understand. This is a vital principle of Scripture, and it is ignored contrary to the will of the Lord. Indeed, to reject this principle combines heartlessness with spiritual disobedience.

5. God directs that children hear the Gospel

A fifth biblical principle which must direct us and shape our work for children, is that the instruction of the young must be primarily and chiefly *evangelistic*. When someone says to me (and this has happened more than once), 'I am following as a Sunday School syllabus the Westminster Confession,' I am a little taken aback, because while it may be possible to handle the Confession in an appropriate way, it seems to me that the speaker has not understood that Sunday Schools are first and foremost supposed to be evangelistic.

The principle that children's instruction should be

primarily (though certainly not exclusively) evangelistic comes directly from the pages of Scripture. In *Exodus 12.25-27,* for example, we read, *It shall come to pass, when ye be come to the land which the Lord will give you, according as he hath promised, that ye shall keep this service* [the Passover]. *And it shall come to pass, when your children shall say unto you, What mean ye by this service? that ye shall say, It is the sacrifice of the Lord's passover, who passed over the houses of the children of Israel in Egypt, when he smote the Egyptians, and delivered our houses.*

What exactly were the children to be taught about the Passover? What did they teach in ancient times, and what is to be the content of the Sunday School lesson today, according to the direction of Scripture? Chiefly, the lesson is to have a *gracious* content, explaining the sacrifice necessary for *deliverance,* and pointing out that only those who believe are saved (for the Lord smote the Egyptians).

The lesson is to be about *deliverance,* a wonderful word which encompasses weakness, lostness, need, rescue by another and consequent safety. The lesson is to be about *the Gospel,* and this is invariably the case when the Old Testament mentions the duty of instructing children – it is a principle of Scripture.

Very similar teaching appears in *Joshua 4.21-24,* when the children of Israel crossed the Jordan, and memorial stones were placed in the midst of the river. It is recorded that Joshua – *spake unto the children of Israel, saying, When your children shall ask their fathers in time to come, saying, What mean these stones? Then ye shall let your children know, saying, Israel came over this Jordan on dry land. For the Lord your God dried up the waters of Jordan from before you, until ye were passed over, as the Lord your God did to the Red sea, which he dried up from before us, until we were gone over: that all the people of the earth might know the hand of the Lord, that it is mighty: that ye might fear the Lord your God for ever.*

There could not be a more evangelistic message than this! It is a lesson about total deliverance being provided by the Lord. He did not help them to wade or swim the waters. He removed the barrier entirely and gave them a secure passage – by His mighty hand. It is a picture of salvation entirely by grace, as opposed to works.

It is a lesson about mercy and grace; about the Lord doing for His people things which they could never do for themselves. It is also about the Red Sea, and about awe and reverence and obedience to God, the only Saviour. The great child-instruction passages of the Old Testament are thoroughly evangelistic in character, and so must our children's ministry be today.

The ongoing pleading of *Deuteronomy 30.19* applied to adults and their children: *I call heaven and earth to record this day against you, that I have set before you life and death, blessing and cursing: therefore choose life, that both thou and thy seed may live.*

Romans 4.11 is a precious and important text in connection with the way in which the rising generation were instructed in Old Testament times. Speaking of Abraham, it tells us – *And he received the sign of circumcision.* All infant boys were to be circumcised as a sign, or lesson. What precisely did this teach? Some say that circumcision was a sign that the child was a member of God's covenant of grace, and this rite therefore taught the special privileges of the children of God. Actually, the Scriptures never say any such thing.

The Scriptures never present circumcision as a sign or badge that anyone was definitely saved, or a member of anything. Circumcision was not a seal of approval or a badge of belonging. It was not a warrant card indicating membership of God's covenant. What was it? Paul tells us: *He received the sign of circumcision, a seal of the righteousness of the faith which he had yet being uncircumcised: that he might be the father of all them that believe.*

What was circumcision intended to teach? It was a sign that said, 'Look at Abraham. Observe how he pleased God, and how he came to be blessed. It was not by his works but by his *faith*; by believing God. This was accounted to him for righteousness.' The sign of circumcision taught the Gospel. It taught the basics. It taught justification by grace *through faith*, just as all the other rites and ceremonies of the Old Testament presented salvation truths.

71

This is important to us, because if God begins the instruction of the young – as babes – with a sign pointing to salvation by faith, this must be the chief aim of our children's instruction also. We are not to make Bible history or geography our chief aim. (Certainly maps and simple historical outlines may assist, but they are secondary.) We are not to major on Bible data, or imitate the approach of secular school religious education. We are to emphasise the themes of law and grace and mercy.

It is a matter of great concern that many Sunday School materials are not particularly evangelistic. In many lesson-aid publications the Gospel comes up only occasionally, and then without any depth of persuasive reasoning. Many such aids do no more than outline Bible 'stories' and often in a light and trivial manner.

The children are not taught the nature and consequences of sin, or the sinfulness and hurtfulness of it. There is scant attention to the graciousness of Christ, and the necessity of salvation.

We need to teach lessons which reflect thorough preparation by teachers who are deeply concerned for the conversion of their children. Our labours must be undergirded by the conviction that it is God Himself Who calls us to emphasise the Gospel to the young.

6. A History of Evangelism of Children

THE PURPOSE of this chapter is to trace something of the history of evangelistic work among young people, with a view to answering the objection, often raised, that the Sunday School is a modern phenomenon.

God has commanded His people to provide a religious education for children. *Train up a child in the way he should go: and when he is old, he will not depart from it (Proverbs 22.6).* Josephus, the Jewish historian, reminds the Jews of this in his *Antiquities*. He writes, 'Let the children also learn the laws, as the first thing they are taught, which will be the best thing they can be taught, and will be the cause of their future felicity.'

As a result of such teaching, the Jews took steps to ensure that in every town a person was appointed for this purpose. 'In every city and town,' observes Dr John Lightfoot, 'there was a school where children were taught to read the law; and if there were any town, where there was not such a school, the men of that place stood excommunicate, till such a one was erected.'

Scripture itself mentions men like Nicodemus who was a 'teacher of Israel' *(John 3.10)*. Gamaliel, a member of the Sanhedrin and an eminent Pharisee, appears to have had his own school at Jerusalem, where Paul, as a Jewish boy, was taught both the Law of Moses and the traditions of the Elders *(Acts 22.3)*.

When the Christian church began, it too had teachers responsible for the instruction of the young. We have in a previous chapter noted the references to 'catechising' in the New Testament. These teachers seem to have used simple 'forms', or outlines of the faith *(Romans 6.17; 2 Timothy 1.13)*, to teach *the first principles of the oracles of God (Hebrews 5.12)*.

Later, in the church of the sub-apostolic age, there were people specially chosen to be catechists. Pantaenus, somewhere around AD 180, founded a catechetical school in Alexandria, where Clement and Origen subsequently taught. Other such schools were established at Rome, Caesarea, Antioch, and Athens. While they came to assume a more learned character as theological colleges, originally they were designed for the purpose of providing basic Christian teaching prior to baptism and church membership.

According to Joseph Bingham, author of *Origines Ecclesiasticae*, 'there were such sort of catechetic schools adjoining to the church in many places.' Bingham quotes the Emperor Leo to the effect that 'they were a sort of building belonging to the church.' It is difficult to conceive of anything more like Sunday Schools!

During the Dark Ages (the period from the late fifth century to about AD 1000), the Church of Rome kept the minds of adults and children in total ignorance of the Truth. But, as Professor Eadie remarks, 'No sooner was the reformed religion established, than provision was made for the instruction of all persons, especially children, in the fundamental doctrines of religion.'

We turn then to the Reformation of the sixteenth century, observing at once that it had three chief branches – the Lutheran in Germany, the Zwinglian and Calvinistic in Switzerland, France, Holland and Scotland, and the Anglican here in England. Now it can be shown that wherever Protestantism took hold, there was a concern expressed for children resulting in a determined effort to reach them with the Word of God.

Take, first of all, the so-called *Lutheran Reformation.* One of Martin Luther's greatest concerns was the true and proper education of children. As early as 1520, in a *Manifesto* delivered 'to the Christian nobility of the German nation', Luther urged the importance of taking the Gospel to them. 'Oh!' he exclaimed, 'How badly we treat that unhappy band of young people entrusted to us for guidance and education. We can hardly justify ourselves for not having set the Word of God before their eyes.'

In 1524, he issued his celebrated call 'to the magistrates of all the German towns', inviting them to set up Christian schools. There he laments the absence of any real desire to reach the young and declares that 'the devil much prefers blockheads and drones.'

Luther's own Short Catechism appeared in 1529. Designed especially for children, to establish them in the reformed faith, it proved to be an exceedingly useful teaching aid. To ministers who might use it he wrote, 'With the young, always keep to one form and teach them word for word *[ie: avoid different versions]* so that the young may repeat and learn them by heart.'

And Luther was speaking from experience here. 'I am a doctor and a teacher,' he once said, 'but I am like a child who is taught the Catechism, and I read and recite *word by word* in the morning the Ten Commandments, the Articles of the Creed, and the Lord's Prayer, and cheerfully remain a child and pupil of the Catechism.'

To quote Dr Philip Schaff, 'The Little Catechism, which is his best, bears the stamp of his religious genius, and is, next to his translation of the Bible, his most useful and enduring work, by which he continues a living teacher in catechetical classes and Sunday Schools as far as the Lutheran confession extends.'

Our Reformer believed that Christian ministers had a

duty to ensure that children were taught the Gospel. Writing to the Elector, John of Saxony, on May 20th, 1530, he gratefully acknowledged that 'the merciful God' was 'making His Word powerful and fruitful. For surely,' he writes, 'your Grace's land has more excellent pastors and preachers than any other land in the whole world.'

What particularly impressed and delighted him, however, was that 'the tender youth, both boys and girls' were 'so well instructed in the Catechism and the Scriptures.' Luther says, 'I am deeply moved when I see that young boys and girls can pray, believe, and speak more of God and Christ than they ever could *[before]*.'

That same year (1530) Luther preached a sermon in which he called for more to be done in this area. 'We must . . . have ordinary pastors,' he said, 'who will teach the Gospel and Catechism to the young, and the ignorant.'

Pastors may not be able, however, to reach the masses. Luther was quick to realise that. He saw that others would need to help, and so he encouraged ordinary church members to take up the work of teaching the young. He once remarked, 'I know that, next to preaching, this is the best, surest, and most useful vocation – and I am not sure which of the two is better; for it is hard to reform old sinners with whom the preacher has to do, while the young tree can be made to bend without breaking.'

In Martin Luther, we have a real enthusiast for child evangelism. His heart *burned* for the salvation of children's souls. This was recognised by Dr Thomas Lindsay, the historian, who said of Luther, 'he desired to give all German children the means of receiving the same evangelical education which he had received from his father and mother.'

Among the faithful, the name of Martin Luther is remembered with honour, not only because he redis-covered and restored biblical truth to the church, but also because he did everything in his power to win others to Christ – especially the young. He was one whose great aim was to train children both for service and for eternity.

Contemporaneous with, but independent of, the Lutheran movement, was the *Zwinglian* or *Calvinistic Reformation.* Ulrich Zwingli began his reforms at Einsiedeln in 1516; but, in 1518, he was called to the office of preacher in the cathedral of Zurich which greatly facilitated the advancement of reform in Swit-zerland. His important essay, *Of the Education of Youth,* was written at Zurich in 1523. Its first part testifies to Zwingli's concern for young people. It tells – 'how the tender mind of youth is to be instructed in the things of God' and, although concentrating on the 'young men who have already attained to discretion', it nevertheless asserts that there are 'directions' which should be given 'from the cradle or during the earliest years'.

Zwingli's remarks are worth noting, emphasising, as they do, the duty of working and praying for the conversion of the young. 'It is necessary,' he says, 'not merely to instil faith into the young people by the pure words which proceed from the mouth of God, but to pray that He Who alone can give faith will illuminate by His Spirit those whom we instruct in His Word.'

Proceeding now to the Calvinistic period, we notice at once that Guillaume Farel, Calvin's predecessor, began his work at Aigle – a village to the south-east of the Lake of Geneva – by opening a school and teaching children the Word of God. History records how the children began to tell their parents about what they were hearing, with the result that the townspeople, one after another, came to Farel asking if he would teach them too. What a development!

I believe it illustrates an important truth: if we are faithful in teaching the children, it may be that we shall be given the opportunity of contacting their parents and even of reaching whole families for the Lord Jesus Christ. *A little child shall lead them (Isaiah 11.6).*

The historian, Dr J. A. Wylie, quoting Ruchart, describes what happened next: 'Through the minds of the children he gained access to those of the parents; and when he had gathered a little flock around him, he threw off his disguise, and announced himself as "William Farel, the Minister".'

Wylie continues, 'Though he had dropped from the

clouds, the priests could not have been more affrighted, nor the people more surprised, than they were at the sudden metamorphosis of the schoolmaster. Farel instantly mounted the pulpit. His bold look, his burning eye, his voice of thunder, his words, rapid, eloquent, and stamped with the majesty of truth, reached the conscience, and increased the number of those in the valley of Aigle who were already prepared to take the Word of God for their guide.'

Farel's acting the part of schoolmaster should not surprise us. As Gabriel Mutzenberg has recently written, 'The line between pastor and schoolteacher was often blurred, for the Bible was both the unique foundation of the reformed faith and the special text for teaching reading.'

Of course, our interest will be particularly with John Calvin. He came to Geneva in July, 1536, and almost immediately prepared a catechism for the instruction of the young. Later, in 1545, he prepared another, *The Catechism of the Church of Geneva*, which John Knox thought the best that had ever been produced. Calvin, in the title, described it as 'a Plan of Instructing Children in the Doctrine of Christ'.

Observing that 'the practice of writing catechisms for the young was general among the churches of the Reformation,' Dr James Stalker made the point that – 'the greatest men of the age, like Luther and Calvin, did not disdain to stoop to this humble task; herein showing their wisdom; for the influence is incalculable which religious truth exerts on the subsequent life when it has been imprinted on the mind in early years.'

Interestingly, Calvin's later catechism is in the form of a dialogue between a minister and a child and, in the French text, it is divided into fifty-five Sunday parts. Calvin believed that ministers had the responsibility for ensuring that children were taught each Lord's Day. In his introduction, he writes, 'It has always been a practice and diligent care of the church, that children be rightly brought up in Christian doctrine.' (Interjecting here, I do wonder what his opinion would be of those modern 'Calvinists' who stubbornly refuse to reach and teach them!)

He continues, 'To do this more conveniently, not only were schools formerly opened and individuals enjoined to teach their families properly, but also it was accepted public custom to examine children in the churches concerning the specific points which should be common and familiar to all Christians.'

On November 20th, 1541, the *Ecclesiastical Ordinances* became law. Intended, as they were, to provide a scheme for a properly ordered church, they required, in addition to the Sunday worship services, children's classes at midday in each of Geneva's three parish churches, Saint Pierre, La Madeleine, and Saint Gervais.

'All citizens and inhabitants are to bring or to convey their *children on Sundays* at midday to Catechism . . . A definite formulary is to be composed by which they will be instructed, and on this, with the teaching given them, they are to be interrogated about what has been said, to see if they have listened and remembered well . . . In order that there be no mistake, let it be ordained that the children who come to school assemble there before twelve o'clock, and that the masters conduct them in good order in each parish.'

Before moving on, mention should be made of John Knox, who promoted the cause of the Calvinistic Reformation in Scotland. When in 1560 the Great Council of the realm commissioned the 'ministers of Christ Jesus' to provide their 'judgements touching the reformation of Religion', the result was a document called the *Book of Discipline*, drawn up by a number of Reformers, among whom John Knox was perhaps the most prominent.

That highly valuable and formative book included among the necessary marks of a true church, 'that the children and rude *[uneducated]* persons be instructed in the chief points of religion.' And, after the Genevan model, it states that 'before noone must the Word be preached and . . . after noone must the yong children be publickly examined in their Catechisme.' Here is yet another example of a sixteenth century Sunday School.

Still in that century, we turn to the *Anglican Reformation*. Naturally, we think first of Thomas Cranmer who, in 1553, published a German catechism entitled, *A*

Short Instruction into the Christian Religion; for the syngular commoditie and profite of children and young people.

While unsatisfactory in certain respects, because not fully reformed, it was nevertheless issued, as Cranmer himself tells us, 'that the yet unskillful in young age' may have 'the foundations laid of religion.'

Writing about it to the king, Edward VI, Cranmer expresses the view that 'commonly as we are in youth brought up, so we continue in age.' He then proceeds to emphasise the importance of impressing 'God's holy Word' on 'tender hearts', concluding with a prayer that 'the youth of your Grace's realm may learn to know God.'

At that time, many of the English clergy were ignorant of the Truth and not a few of them were hostile to the Reformation. Awareness of this led Bishop John Hooper, in 1551-2, to draw up fifty articles, to which he required all his ministers to subscribe. Article 31 states, 'that the catechism be read and taught unto the children every Sunday . . . at one or two of the clock after dinner, and that they may be thereof duly examined one after another by order.'

An appended document required that 'parsons, vicars, and curates . . . that be not weekly occupied with preaching, teach and bring up the youth and children of theirs or their parishioners in the catechism and rudiments or principles of their faith.'

Similar were Archbishop Grindal's *Injunctions for the Clergy* (1571). This good man, sympathetic to Puritanism, ordered all ministers 'every Sunday . . . in church or chapel . . . to instruct the children,' and he was certainly in earnest, for he added, 'to the intent this thing may be more effectually executed, ye shall take the names of all the children . . . in your parish, that be above six years of age and under twenty.' Now this is 1571, and local churches are being urged to teach all the children round about them.

If Grindal was sympathetic to Puritanism, Archbishop John Whitgift certainly was not. Yet even he believed that 'the dissoluteness in manners, and ignorance in the common sort, that reigneth in most parts of this realm' would be effectively redressed by 'catechizing, and instructing in churches, of youths of both sexes, on the sabbath-days . . . in afternoons.' (This is from *A Letter to the Bishops of the Province*, 1591.)

The 59th Canon of the 101st *Constitutions and Canons Ecclesiastical* of 1603 was very explicit and binding on 'every parson, vicar, and curate' upon 'every Sunday' for 'half an hour or more' to 'instruct the youth.' It added, 'If any minister neglect his duty herein, let him be *sharply* reproved.'

After the Reformers, came that noble company of Puritans who felt the same burden for the conversion of children. 'Dear lambs,' exclaims Thomas Lye, directly addressing them in one of his sermons, 'the Searcher of hearts knows how greatly I long after you all in the bowels of Jesus Christ . . . O what a credit, what a glory, is it to drink in the dews of godliness in the morning of your lives! . . . On the other side, how dangerous are delays! Remember children, late repentance, like untimely fruits, seldom comes to anything . . . As young as you are, you may be old enough for a grave . . . O then seek your God, and seek Him when and *while He may be found.*'

Puritans believed in evangelising children. Let no one deny it! Listen to Matthew Henry, preaching in 1713: 'Let the ministers of Christ look upon themselves as under a charge to feed the lambs of Christ's flock. *All the reformed churches* make this *a part of their work*; to be done either publicly or privately; either in their solemn religious assemblies, or in meetings on purpose for this work . . .

'O that we who are ministers, were filled with a *zeal for the spiritual welfare and eternal salvation of young people*, and a concern for the rising generation; and were to do our utmost, as our ability and opportunity is, to fill the minds of young ones, in their early days, with the knowledge of Christ, and to fix them for Christ, that the next generation may be better than this! . . .

'Let us look with pity upon the great numbers of children, even in our land, who are not taught these forms of sound words, but are bred up in ignorance and profaneness; strangers and enemies to Christ, and true

Christianity. They are *poor, they are foolish, for they know not the way of the Lord, nor the judgment of their God.* If you can do anything, sirs, have compassion upon them and help them; pick up some of those abandoned young ones, you who have ability, and rescue them from ruin, by putting them into a way of receiving instruction.'

What they preached, they were careful to put into practice. This may be seen in the case of Joseph Alleine who, his biographer tells us, 'always had a school of sixty or seventy poor children at his lodgings on Sundays, to receive Christian instruction.' Alleine's wife, Theodosia, tells us 'they profited much by his instructions.'

Others, not strictly Puritans, also believed in singling out the young for special attention. There was John Bunyan, for example. He wrote *A Book for Boys and Girls*, a lengthy poem designed to inculcate Gospel truth. One of the lines in that poem has Bunyan saying, 'I would be catching boys and girls.' I wonder if each of us could say that?

We say, 'I would be in my study,' and 'I would be preaching sermons,' and 'I would be building up my congregation,' and 'I would be reforming the church,' and 'I would be sitting on committees,' but John Bunyan says – 'I would be catching boys and girls.'

Benjamin Keach, a former minister of the church now known as the Metropolitan Tabernacle, was sentenced in 1664 to a fine, imprisonment and pillory for writing his book for the spiritual instruction of children. When all copies of the book were destroyed, he rewrote it from memory and subsequently it ran into a number of editions. 'It reveals,' as Dr A. C. Underwood once observed, 'the interest Baptists were taking in the winning of the young.'

A little later, it was the turn of Isaac Watts. He wrote his famous *Divine and Moral Songs for Children.*

Mention has already been made of Alleine's Sunday School. But did you ever hear of John Brown of Priesthill? He was the Covenanter whom Claverhouse had cruelly murdered before his wife and children in 1685. This dear man regularly gathered children around him on Sunday evenings in order to teach them the way of God's salvation.

Another Scot, David Lambert (Boston's successor at Ettrick), is said to have taught a Sunday School in Berkshire, 'highly spoken of for its blessed effects', as early as 1710.

A study of the seventeenth and early eighteenth centuries will make one thing very clear: determined efforts were being made throughout this period to evangelise children. It was, I believe, an integral part of true Puritanism.

Although our study shows there were Sunday Schools long before Robert Raikes's school was opened in 1783, this should not lead us to underestimate that man's achievement. Raikes tells us how he was led to introduce his particular scheme. 'I was struck with concern,' he says, 'at seeing a group of children, wretchedly ragged, at play in the streets. I asked an inhabitant whether those children belonged to that part of the town, and lamented their misery and idleness.

' "Ah! sir," said the woman to whom I was speaking, "could you take a view of this part of the town on a Sunday, you would be shocked indeed; for then the street is filled with multitudes of these wretches, who, released on that day from employment, spend their time in noise and riot, playing at 'chuck', and cursing and swearing in a manner so horrid as to convey to any serious mind an idea of hell rather than any other place." '

Years later, writing to Joseph Lancaster, Raikes said, 'I can never pass by the spot where the word "try" came so powerfully into my mind, without lifting up my heart and hands to heaven in gratitude to God for having put such a thought into my head.'

One cannot help being reminded here of what is said in the Gospel of our Saviour. *He was moved with compassion on them, because they . . . were . . . as sheep having no shepherd (Matthew 9.36).*

Would that we all knew that compassion! Raikes was 'struck with concern'. So should we be when, on the Lord's Day, we see children gathering in our streets, riding their bicycles, and playing games. Many of them know nothing of God's love. They have never heard of the Redeemer, and they are living in a way which can only lead to eternal ruin. How can we ignore them? Brethren and sisters, pray that you too will be 'struck with concern'. That word 'try' may then come into your minds.

In a history of Sunday Schools, a conclusion devoted to motives and incentives will not be amiss. Reflect for a few moments upon this question: Why have Christians in every age insisted on giving children a knowledge of the Bible?

The *first* answer must be that the Lord Jesus, in His great last commission, commanded His disciples to *Go . . . and preach the gospel to every creature (Mark 16.15)*. Christ's church must therefore be evangelistic, taking His message to *every creature*: literally, 'to the whole creation', the whole world of men, women, *and children*. It is to our shame if we fail in this and allow non-Christian schoolteachers to attempt it instead. If you are a reformed minister, I must ask you: When was the last time you, or someone from your church, spoke to the children of your area?

Secondly, it is tragically possible for us to wrong children's souls. We may recall the words of *Genesis 42.22, Do not sin against the child*. If we do not tell them of Jesus Christ, a fate worse than death will befall them. As Dr C. G. Trumbull once said, 'If the church of Christ doesn't look after these children, the devil will.'

Thirdly, when the Lord's people have been faithful in their task, they have often witnessed the manifestation of God's power, with converts multiplied in flourishing churches. Dr John Donne, Dean of St Paul's, asserted what even Papists had to concede, that at the time of the Reformation the Protestants gained great advantage by their catechising of children.

The infamous Council of Trent (1545-63) spoke of 'the mischief which the Protestants have done the [*Roman*] Catholic Church, not only by their tongues, but especially by their writings called "catechisms".' O that more mischief were done to that Roman Antichrist!

Fourthly, some methods of evangelism are difficult to employ and they often fail to produce results, but it is relatively easy to gather children together. While the adult Jews in our Lord's day showed little interest, the children were willing to assemble in the Temple, and sing, *Hosanna to the son of David (Matthew 21.15).*

Fifthly, the influence of the Sunday School has been felt in the lives of millions. Its fruits are *beyond* human reckoning. How can we account for that? There is, of course, the factor of divine sovereignty. But something else should be considered. Children, although sinners, are not yet hardened in sin, as they will be. Young children are, as John Cotton once pointed out, 'flexible and easily bowed. It is far more easy to train them up to good things now, than in their youth and riper years.'

Sixthly, there are special promises concerning the young, such as, *Those that seek me early* [literally, in the morning] *shall find me (Proverbs 8.17)*. Early life is the very best time to seek the Lord. John Wesley enthused over the Sunday Schools which he found springing up everywhere. In 1784, he wrote, 'Perhaps God may have a deeper end thereto than men are aware of. Who knows but what some of these schools may become nurseries for Christians!'

Seventhly, the children around us will soon be the men and women of our nation. Our responsibility is to train up a race of holy men and women, to preserve the church in this land. In this, we work with God Whose gracious design is to perpetuate *a godly seed (Malachi 2.15)*.

Eighthly, by teaching young people in Sunday Schools we will be doing something to check the rising tide of error. Children are being taught that the Bible can no longer be regarded as the Word of God. Its account of creation, for example, is said to contain a collection of myths and legends belonging to Hebrew folklore. As an alternative, evolution is uninhibitedly presented as absolute fact. At the present time, the situation is such that in most British schools children are being taught Hinduism, Buddhism, Islam, and other world religions at the expense of biblical Christianity. But in our Sunday Schools we have a marvellous opportunity to teach children the Truth.

Ninthly, our prayer has often been for revival, but who knows what ministers and missionaries God may raise up in our Schools? We are told that men like Henderson, Patterson, and Morrison, who did such great work for Christ's cause in other lands, received their first spiritual impressions in such places. How that should encourage you teachers! You are doing a great work. It may be that you will secure for the church another Calvin, a Whitefield, a Carey, or a Judson.

Tenthly, remember that death visits the young as well as the old. Job, David, and Jeroboam, were all fathers who lost children. Commenting upon *Ecclesiastes 3.2*, Matthew Henry writes, 'Some observe that here is *a time to be born and a time to die*, but no time to live; that is so short that it is not worth mentioning.'

The next great event after death will be the judgement when, according to the Bible's last book, *the dead, SMALL and great* will stand before God *(Revelation 20.12)*. The reference is to age as well as rank. *Children* will be judged. In the light of that solemn fact, we are called to teach them the Gospel and provide them with a saving plea which, on that great and terrible day, will prevail to everlasting life.

May God stir us afresh to work and pray for the conversion of children so that we may one day rejoice to see many of them in the heavenly kingdom!

7. How to Gather and Teach Them

But God hath chosen the foolish things of the world to confound the wise; and God hath chosen the weak things of the world to confound the things which are mighty; and base things of the world, and things which are despised, hath God chosen, yea, and things which are not, to bring to nought things that are: that no flesh should glory in his presence (1 Corinthians 1.27-29).

GRACE IS WONDERFULLY exalted in the conversion of children. Spurgeon used to say that nothing tears down the pride of Satan as much as the conversion of a child – for God chooses *things which are not, to bring to nought things that are.*

For Satan to lose his prey, when that prey is a vulnerable child, is for him a great humiliation. He hates to see the praise of youngsters directed towards Almighty God. Conversion means that Satan, for all his considerable intelligence, is unable to deceive even the little children. They come to see through his deceptions, and they see him for what he is.

God is glorified, and as God is glorified, Satan is degraded. It is not surprising therefore, that Sunday Schools and Sunday School workers should be the enemy and target of Satan. Nor is it surprising that Satan should tempt God's people into thinking that Sunday Schools are not worthwhile.

Believers often express a certain amount of pity for pastors. 'Oh,' they say, 'the minister of God, the preacher of God's Word, must be under particular attack from the enemy. He must have to fight extraordinary battles.' But the same goes for Sunday School teachers, for they are called to inflict upon the devil the most humbling defeats of all.

Anyone who brings children to worship God, and to seek Him, will do so against a tide of satanic discouragement and obstruction. Theirs is a great and costly ministry, and for this reason it deserves the protection and the prayers of the whole church.

But how are children to be gathered and taught? This chapter will range across a number of practical recommendations for the encouragement of those who engage in Sunday School work. It will by no means be a complete or adequate treatment of how to go about the ministry of the Sunday School, but will, hopefully, furnish some help and stimulation.

The first practical suggestion concerns a method of gathering children which has passed over the last thirty years from being a profitable innovation to an absolute necessity. These days we really must *transport* the majority of the children. In most areas of Britain this is now the secret of large Sunday Schools. Size will depend on whether we 'pied piper' and transport the scholars.

How many cars are there in our church? The work of transporting children is wonderful for car owners. It removes idolatry at a stroke! Appeal to church members to take a regular responsibility – a regular route.

Most churches can afford a minibus or two for such a vital outreach, and these may be augmented by as many private cars as the members can muster. The writer first saw such a scheme operated by a church in the Midlands over twenty-five years ago, and was deeply impressed by the huge Sunday School which resulted.

One of the arguments in favour of an afternoon Sunday School (though this may not be advantageous in all areas) is the fact that many church members can be mobilised to the task of transportation.

Quite apart from transportation, something needs to be done these days even for those children who live within walking distance, because there are so many distractions, and children are fickle. Faithful believers need to go round the streets every Sunday, knocking the doors where enrolled scholars live, and leading bands of children to church. These are the 'pied pipers', and they, like the minibus and car teams, get to know the children and their homes very well.

Then, of course, the children must be speedily registered as they arrive at Sunday School. Apart from the necessary efficiency, especially in the proper recording of all newcomers, this procedure has a great effect upon the children. They respect it, and it settles them. As they arrive, they realise that things are being properly and systematically done from the very beginning, even before they are ushered into the hall, and this promotes respect. Absentees should be promptly followed up by teachers or department leaders. A Sunday School will grow only if it is supported by conscientious visitation.

The advice of this writer is – recruit scholars constantly! On no account lapse into occasional recruiting, resorting to annual events such as 'holiday clubs'. I would not say anything to discourage such clubs in areas where they prove helpful, but if recruiting depends upon them, there may be a high price to pay.

There is considerable advantage (especially in 'working class' districts) in recruiting to Sunday School *all the time*, so that new children arrive in a constant flow or steady trickle. When this is the case, these new children – who are much in the minority – readily adapt to the prevailing atmosphere. And if we have achieved reverent behaviour and good attention, then it will be secure.

How are new children likely to react to the strange and different environment of Sunday School? What will they make of worship, and prayers and Bible instruction? The answer is, they will usually adapt to the behaviour of the overwhelming majority, listening, singing and praying with the crowd. It can be a sad blow to that reverent, listening atmosphere, probably built up over many years, when sixty new children recruited in the holiday club come in together! My cordial advice is – treasure that hard-won atmosphere, take no risks, and recruit all the time.

This leads us naturally to consider the *atmosphere* of the Sunday School. Reverence is so important. For the leading of the Sunday School departments we must select those people who can best manage the children. And we must also remember the importance of 'pace'.

In adult services it is right for us to be a little on the slow side in our worship. Most of us who are conservative in worship like a small pause, for example, after a prayer, before the minister announces the next hymn. We favour time to think, and we dislike being rushed through the elements of the service with indecent haste.

We recognise, however, that in the Sunday School the standard is quite different. The rule is that you do not give the children one half-second to breathe or to think! Their minds must not wander from the track, and so the service must move swiftly from one item to the next. If sister Kate is to read the Bible portion, make sure she knows that she must be up at the front by the time you have finished making the announcements. If she does not begin her long stroll until your last sentence has died away, there will be a long pause, and the attention (or the reverence) of the children may be lost. There must be *pace*, with one thing leading immediately to another, in the Sunday School, to sustain attention, order, and reverence.

Another piece of advice which has been handed down through generations of Sunday School workers concerns discipline. Sometimes you find Sunday Schools as well as children's weeknight meetings seriously flawed because the leaders are much too lenient towards one child, or perhaps a number of children, who behave extremely badly. One or two children may be allowed to wreck everything because the leader is reluctant to take them home and say to the parents, 'I am sorry, but we cannot cope with your lad at present. Perhaps he could try again next year.'

Facing the facts not only saves a class from uselessness, but it may be best for the child. If we are not succeeding in getting our spoken message over to a badly behaved child in class, the fact that he or she is to be shut out of the School and its activities until behaviour improves may be the best form of 'message'. Through this the child will hear the *law* if not the Gospel!

The matter of discipline brings us to consider a vital

method in Sunday School work. We must have a 'fishing net' approach. A Sunday School (particularly an urban one) is like a great net being trawled through the sea. The object of the exercise is to trawl and catch as many fish as we can.

Sometimes Sunday Schools work with only a small net, transferring a few fish to a garden pond, where they then devote their entire attention to those few fish. You may have a class of, say, ten children, and three go absent and four misbehave. You put all your work for months, even years, into getting the same children back again and again, calming them down and giving them yet another chance. And while all your time and energy is spent on the few, a thousand unchurched children in the town remain neglected.

We must accept that some children will stop coming, and after reasonable attempts have been made to bring them back, we may have to give them up, and replace them with others. Some will behave extremely badly, and abuse several 'further chances' to improve. Then, we may have to give them up.

We are a fishing net, remember, and multitudes must be reached. Do not extend excessive consideration to the existing few names on the register at the expense of bringing in new ones. The principle of focusing on homes where we receive a hearing, and knowing when to leave the obdurate (as taught by Christ in the sending of the twelve and the seventy) must guide us here.

What about the Sunday School teacher's own performance? What should a teacher aim for, and what pitfalls should be avoided? It is important to remember that every Sunday School teacher is an evangelist, a pastor, an example and a friend to children, and all these roles must be fulfilled.

If you are a teacher, you are certainly first and foremost an evangelist. The loss of this conviction has been the beginning of failure for many a teacher (and many a School). But you are also a pastor-teacher to those who seek and find the Lord. Many young converts will not have Christian parents, and you will be God's appointed person to feed their souls, counsel and guide them.

It is a sobering thought to remember that you are an example, and children notice everything! They observe you, and they discern both your qualities and your faults. No one is as observant of human character as a child. You must never lose your temper. You must never behave in a way that would bring dishonour to the cause, or put off the children. You are an evangelist, a pastor, *and* an example of the transforming power of conversion. Your demeanour and deportment is a lesson in itself. The very tone of your voice when you call a child to order says a lot to that child about your character.

Never forget you are appointed by the Friend of sinners to be a *friend* to your children. Pray to God to give you a friendly heart. Pray that you will have affection and care for them, and that this will show. Then visit them when they fall by the wayside.

We need to have a real affection for our children. The cold individual who serves out of duty only is an encumbrance to the work. Weeknight meetings are so valuable here. Do not organise them as mere baits. Arrange them as an additional means of getting alongside your children and teenagers, to talk and witness to them. And whatever the activities, always have a good, strong spiritual-meeting-element, following a well-constructed plan.

The ideal Sunday School teacher constantly examines himself about the quality of his teaching. You must be self-critical to be a capable teacher. How did that lesson go? What did I do wrong? What is the matter with my teaching that I lose the attention of the group? In what way can I improve it? An able person, who is also rather proud, can never be as effective as a less able person who practises self-examination, and who strives for self-improvement.

The good Sunday School teacher aims at *interesting* the children. He never speaks *at* the children, or even worse, across the top of the children, but *to* the children. He is always acutely aware of how much attention he is being given, for the response matters to him. If he is not getting through, he alters his tone, inserts an illustration, or adopts some strategy for recapturing interest and attention. He is not a dull, dry lecturer, but seeks to master his class rather like a person playing an instrument. He gets to know what he must do to keep eyes bright, heads up, and hands still.

A keen Sunday School teacher will be concerned about the voice, and this is not an artificial matter. He will ask himself, 'Is my voice monotonous and boring?' There are many people who make lively conversationalists, but the instant you call upon them to do something in a formal way, such as giving an address or teaching a class, their voice becomes dull and flat.

This certainly happens to preachers. Some of the most boring preachers this writer has heard are extremely animated and interesting in personal conversation. How often one thinks – 'Is there anything one can do to help him to carry that natural liveliness into the pulpit?'

Quite often the loss of fluency and liveliness is due to a lack of preparation, and if this fault is persistent it will leave an indelible scar on the capacity of the teacher to communicate well. If preparation is rushed, the mind is left struggling to manage the message, and there are no spare brain cells for liberty of expression. Poor preparation also leads to habits of desperation, such as the constant repetition of texts or favourite and well-worn expressions. It also leads to teachers being over-sensitive to every disturbance in class. Instead of overcoming unrest with the power of interest, they constantly break off to chastise restless youngsters.

Returning to the voice, every teacher should take stock, from time to time, of his or her tone of voice. Do you lapse into a monotone in class, or does your voice rise and fall as it should? There must be life and expression in our presentation.

A good Sunday School teacher will avoid always *drum-banging*, which is a harmful habit particularly prevalent with youth-class teachers. The drum-banger is the teacher who is always on about the same thing. Every time a pop star commits suicide, the children know they are in for a rough time. They know that this is going to be the inspiration for a long tirade. Every time there is a national disaster or tragedy they know they will get twenty minutes on the nearness of death and the terrors of hell. We must avoid corny and predictable drum-banging. Children have a knack of remembering what we said 'last time' better than we do.

It is important that we do not preach at the children. Sometimes this happens in Sunday School: you hear of a class of five or six children with a fully grown man standing three or four feet away, and bellowing at them. Do be careful to be more friendly and intimate. For small to average classes it is better for the teacher to sit than to stand, unless it really cramps expression.

Also, remember eye contact! Look at your children. Look at them and keep in touch with them. This is the 'language' of friendliness, sincerity and urgency. It is also a helpful encouragement to the children to keep their attention upon you. When the teacher's eyes are fixed on the floor, ceiling or walls, the lesson will only be fractionally useful.

One of the oldest pieces of Sunday School advice 'in the book' is – always have a 'Plan B'. Never go into a Sunday School class without one. When the children become glassy-eyed, and their minds are plainly else-where, or when your lesson has got into a hopeless muddle and there is no getting back on course, the only remedy is to have something in reserve. This may be an illustration or an anecdote, or a word of testimony which you can immediately bring out, and which is bound to cause children to raise their heads and pay rapt attention.

Such a strategy is essential because we cannot let our children learn to ignore us. The old-time teachers developed a little arsenal of items to fall back on when in trouble, and so should we. Even if our presentation has got into such a state that our 'Plan B' has no logical relationship at all to the main subject, it is better to use it than to continue in disaster. Sometimes we have to do this even in preaching – and if no one notices a dis-connection in the material it just shows how much the 'Plan B' was needed! Always have a 'Plan B' in reserve.

It has been emphasised already that our Sunday School lesson should be primarily evangelistic, and this is very hard. The most difficult department of ministry is evangelism.

Admittedly, it is easy to teach the same 'thumbnail' Gospel every week. But to press home the Gospel properly, dealing with different aspects of sin and unbelief, touching upon all the wonders of salvation, maintaining a fresh and challenging emphasis week after week is a very difficult thing.

This is why many pastors are seldom evangelistic. It is why the majority of materials prepared for Sunday School and youth work do not excel in Gospel presentation. It is much easier to teach other doctrines, and to give general biblical instruction, than it is to be regularly evangelistic.

Be careful to do justice to the great biblical concepts of sin and of punishment. There are some things which, in our present society, children do not understand unless they are carefully explained. Today's children do not understand the notion of punishment. They think it is vindictive revenge! They regard it as something ugly, vicious and primitive.

Moderate punishment, which is aimed at correction, they can understand. But punishment from God, and hell, is outside their cultural programming. They can also see a purpose in punishment as a deterrent, but retribution they recoil from. If, therefore, we are to be successful in presenting the need of grace, and the wrath of God, we will need to begin by extolling the righteousness of punishment, and the holiness and justice of God.

Another matter to be stressed constantly is Calvary. Over the years the writer has been amazed to hear that friends who have come to speak at Sunday School anniversaries and prize-givings have frequently omitted any reference to Calvary! Is it not amazing that we can slip so easily into the fundamental error of presenting the Gospel without Calvary!

In all the attention that we give to making visual aids – vital as they are – and to creating a novel 'package' for the lesson, we may forget Calvary! Let us never take for granted the very heart of the Gospel, and the greatest demonstration of the amazing love of Christ.

Make sure, too, that all your work is worthy of respect. Accommodating ourselves to children does not mean we become banal, trite and babyish. If you are babyish in your presentation, and your illustrations are juvenile, and your explanation is over-simplified, then as the children develop in intellect they will despise you and what you teach.

Never forget we represent the great God of Heaven. We are seeking to promote reverence and great respect for the deep mercies of God. So while we accommodate to the age of the child, expressing things simply, we must not over-simplify. Great care is called for in this.

And then teachers must never descend into 'mere story telling', as Spurgeon called it. You must never give the impression that the contents of the Scripture are *stories*. (My wife has campaigned for years to ban the word *story* because of what it means to a child.) We are teaching *reality*, not fiction! The events in the Bible really happened.

We must certainly avoid *christianising* the children. This is the mistaken assumption that as we teach God's Word, the children will gradually become Christians. As time goes by the teacher increasingly treats them as 'insiders', although there has been no spiritual crisis. The teacher's strong desire for the spiritual good of the children may be the cause of this over-optimism and presumption, but it is foolish romanticism. The essence of evangelism is to keep the issues and the terms of entry to the kingdom plainly and clearly before the class, and never to fudge or to encourage presumption on their part. Tender-hearted teachers sometimes greatly err in this matter.

A word of warning may prove helpful to those who prepare Bible-study materials for the use of children. There is a tendency these days to go for ninety per cent pictures, puzzles and interest items, with only ten per cent explanation and application of Scripture. It should, of course, be the other way round. Certainly we must accommodate ourselves to the children, and work to present the Truth in an interesting way. There is nothing wrong with diagrams, pictures to colour, word puzzles and so on. But these must not eclipse the applied presentation of the Word itself.

A few years ago someone passed me a publication to

help children read the Bible, asking for an assessment. It seemed to be very sound, but it was chiefly clever presentation, with only a small amount of serious Bible explanation. I marvelled at the enormous amount of work involved in the excellent execution of 'peripherals'. There was seemingly endless ingenuity and intelligence in the interest themes, puzzles, word games and so on. The publication was a gushing fountain of surprises. But when it came to the explanation and application of the Word, there was no more than any child could understand or see for himself. We must try to hold a better balance, or we shall never accomplish what we set out to do for the Lord. Our first aim is to bring to life the Word of God, and to apply it to human hearts.

In all our labours we must hold before us the fact that children can and will be saved by the power of God operating through the Gospel word. We read in *Matthew 21.15-16*:–

And when the chief priests and scribes saw the wonderful things that he did, and the children crying in the temple, and saying, Hosanna to the son of David; they were sore displeased, and said unto him, Hearest thou what these say? And Jesus saith unto them, Yea; have ye never read, Out of the mouth of babes and sucklings thou hast perfected praise? The quotation of the Lord is from *Psalm 8*, and it assures us that little children are among the elect, and may praise Him perfectly. The old writers love to point out the divine sarcasm in the passage, when the Lord says – *Yea; have ye never read…?* These, remember, were the chief priests and the scribes. They had read everything! They were the experts. What does the Lord mean – *Have ye never read?*

O, they had read that psalm often enough as they led the worship in the synagogues. They had no doubt preached on it, and explained it on numerous occasions. But they had never *read* it; that is to say, they had never *seen* it, or grasped its meaning.

Many erudite reformed preachers are in the same position today. They claim to know a great deal about the Scripture, but we have to challenge them with the words of the Lord – Have you never seen this? Have you not noticed the great compassion of the Lord for children? Have you not seen the possibility of the children in your town being converted through child evangelism?

God is glorified wonderfully in the conversion of young people right down to the little children, because in child conversion His power is shown in so many ways. Of course, the power of God is made glorious when sinners of any age are brought to salvation. But look at the peculiar circumstances of the little child. Consider the fickleness of the child. Is not the wonderful power of God shown, in that He can solemnise the heart and arouse the conscience of even the most fickle? Think of the limited intellect of a little child, and yet the

Spirit of the Lord can impart the essence of saving doctrine to the youngest listener.

Look at the child's natural delight in fun and in self. The things that matter to a child are things that he can have to eat or to enjoy. And yet the power of God can override this dominating instinct for fun and for immediate gratification and bring children to hunger and thirst for pardon and salvation.

A little child has such limited seriousness, and such a short attention span, and yet the power of God can cause that child to carry a convicting word in his heart for days, and to earnestly seek for blessing. These are amazing things. God is wonderfully glorified in the salvation of little children.

And the grace of God is also magnified. Ours is the only religion in the world which rests upon the principle of grace. No wonder God loves the salvation of little children. They are so small, what can they do to merit eternal glory? What can they achieve? What noble, great or wonderful works can they accomplish? They are just little children. And for these reasons they are the perfect candidates for a demonstration of amazing grace.

Children are capable of deep repentance. They have been known to sob themselves to sleep thinking of their sin, and longing to know Christ. And little children can have pure and deep faith, absolute faith in the Gospel and in the Word of God. They can come to love Christ, receive the new nature, and become so different from other children. They can stand, by grace, clear from sin and temptation.

Little children can have patience and endure affliction for Christ. We read of little children stricken down by mortal illness, comforting their parents with spiritual assurances and promises. And little children can serve the Lord. Indeed, they can be more loyal to the Lord than some long-standing church members! The power of God's grace and His converting love can be wonderfully manifested in children.

Converted children can show great courage. Even the naturally timid can resist peer group pressure, and be bold to correct their teachers. Spurgeon used to refer to the converted boy who went to Smithfield to see the burning of martyrs. When he walked back to his neighbourhood, a critical adult asked him where he had been. 'To Smithfield? Why were you there boy? What is a boy doing at Smithfield watching the burnings?' The lad's reply was – 'Sir, I went there to learn the way.' In his young mind he was willing, if it ever came to it, to yield up his life for the Lord.

Sunday School teachers are front line missionaries these days. If you are a teacher, every week you speak to five, ten, or fifteen unconverted souls. You will need the fruit of the Spirit – love, joy, peace, long-suffering, gentleness, goodness, faith (or faithfulness), meekness, and temperance (which is self-control). May the Lord powerfully bless every teacher!

Let us increase our visiting; pray more for our children; take more care in our preparation; and plead more fervently with children to seek the Lord.

May God encourage His people once again to see the possibility of reaching an entire rising generation. May His power rest upon every collector of children, every driver, every helper, every teacher and upon every pastor who faithfully organises, oversees and encourages a Sunday School. May God bless and defend all who serve as defenders, protectors, and deliverers of children! Such people have great significance. May they all be kept in health, and in assurance, and in vigour and diligence!

May pastors never take their eyes off the Sunday School. May they champion its facilities, hire buildings if need be, encourage elders and deacons to share their responsibility and concern, and stir up the people to pray and labour.

To all readers not engaged in Sunday School work – may you be challenged to give yourself to this work, perhaps to resuscitate a Sunday School or to organise one. Give the Lord your heart, your car and your time, and pray to be used to bring in the next generation, and to see Christ glorified in countless childhood conversions. May God re-ignite the vision for *real* Sunday Schooling in our land.